HOUGHTON MIFFLIN HARCOURT

JOURNEYS

Teaching Resources

Kindergarten

HOUGHTON MIFFLIN HARCOURT
School Publishers

Printed in the U.S.A.

ISBN 978-0-54-725400-5

1 2 3 4 5 6 7 8 9 0928 17 16 15 14 13 12 11 10

Contents

Unit 1 Friendly Faces

LESSON 1

BLM 1: Letter Names: Letters *Aa–Ee*
BLM 2: Words to Know: *I*
BLM 3: Letter Names: Letters *Ff–Jj*
BLM 4: Comprehension: Main Ideas
BLM 5: Letter Names: Letters *Kk–Oo*

LESSON 2

BLM 6: Words to Know: *like*
BLM 7: Comprehension: Understanding Characters
BLM 8: Letter Names: Letters *Pp–Tt*

LESSON 3

BLM 9: Words to Know: *the*
BLM 10: Comprehension: Story Structure
BLM 11: Letter Names: Letters *Uu–Zz*
BLM 12: Phonemic Awareness: Letter *Mm*

LESSON 4

BLM 13: Words to Know: *and*
BLM 14: Comprehension: Text and Graphic Features
BLM 15: Phonemic Awareness: Letter *Mm*
BLM 16: Phonics: Letter *Mm*
BLM 17: Phonemic Awareness: Letter *Ss*

LESSON 5

BLM 18: Words to Know: *I, like, the, and*
BLM 19: Comprehension: Sequence of Events
BLM 20: Phonemic Awareness: Letter *Ss*
BLM 21: Phonics: Letter *Ss*
BLM 22: Phonemic Awareness: Letter *Aa*

Unit 2 Show and Tell

LESSON 6

BLM 23: Words to Know: *see*
BLM 24: Comprehension: Compare and Contrast
BLM 25: Phonemic Awareness: Letter *Aa*
BLM 26: Phonics: Letter *Aa*
BLM 27: Phonemic Awareness: Letter *Tt*

LESSON 7

BLM 28: Words to Know: *we*
BLM 29: Comprehension: Understanding Characters
BLM 30: Phonemic Awareness: Letter *Tt*
BLM 31: Phonics: Letter *Tt*
BLM 32: Phonemic Awareness: Letter *Cc*

LESSON 8

BLM 33: Words to Know: *a*
BLM 34: Comprehension: Details
BLM 35: Phonemic Awareness: Letter *Cc*
BLM 36: Phonics: Letter *Cc*
BLM 37: Phonemic Awareness: Letter *Pp*

LESSON 9

BLM 38: Words to Know: *to*
BLM 39: Comprehension: Text and Graphic Features
BLM 40: Phonemic Awareness: Letter *Pp*
BLM 41: Phonics: Letter *Pp*
BLM 42: Phonemic Awareness: Letters *Mm, Ss, Aa, Tt, Cc, Pp*

LESSON 10

BLM 43: Words to Know: *see, we, a, to*
BLM 44: Comprehension: Story Structure
BLM 45: Phonemic Awareness: Letters *Mm, Ss, Aa, Tt, Cc, Pp*
BLM 46: Phonics: Letters *Mm, Ss, Aa, Tt, Cc, Pp*
BLM 47: Phonemic Awareness: Letter *Aa*

Unit 3 Outside My Door

LESSON 11

BLM 48: Words to Know: *come, me*
BLM 49: Comprehension: Compare and Contrast
BLM 50: Phonemic Awareness: Letter *Aa*
BLM 51: Phonics: Letter *Aa*
BLM 52: Phonemic Awareness: Letter *Nn*

LESSON 12

BLM 53: Words to Know: *with, my*
BLM 54: Comprehension: Draw Conclusions
BLM 55: Phonemic Awareness: Letter *Nn*
BLM 56: Phonics: Letter *Nn*
BLM 57: Phonemic Awareness: Letter *Ff*

LESSON 13

BLM 58: Words to Know: *you, what*
BLM 59: Comprehension: Author's Purpose
BLM 60: Phonemic Awareness: Letter *Ff*
BLM 61: Phonics: Letter *Ff*
BLM 62: Phonemic Awareness: Letter *Bb*

LESSON 14

BLM 63: Words to Know: *are, now*
BLM 64: Comprehension: Cause and Effect
BLM 65: Phonemic Awareness: Letter *Bb*
BLM 66: Phonics: Letter *Bb*
BLM 67: Phonemic Awareness: Blend Phonemes

LESSON 15

BLM 68: Words to Know: *come, me, with, my, you, what, are, now*
BLM 69: Comprehension: Sequence of Events
BLM 70: Phonemic Awareness: Blend Phonemes
BLM 71: Phonics: Blend Words
BLM 72: Phonemic Awareness: Letter *Ii*

Unit 4 Let's Find Out

LESSON 16

BLM 73: Words to Know: *is, how*
BLM 74: Comprehension: Details
BLM 75: Phonemic Awareness: Letter *Ii*
BLM 76: Phonics: Letter *Ii*
BLM 77: Phonemic Awareness: Letter *Gg*

LESSON 17

BLM 78: Words to Know: *find, this*
BLM 79: Comprehension: Draw Conclusions
BLM 80: Phonemic Awareness: Letter *Gg*
BLM 81: Phonics: Letter *Gg*
BLM 82: Phonemic Awareness: Letter *Rr*

LESSON 18

BLM 83: Words to Know: *will, be*
BLM 84: Comprehension: Author's Purpose
BLM 85: Phonemic Awareness: Letter *Rr*
BLM 86: Phonics: Letter *Rr*
BLM 87: Phonemic Awareness: Letter *Dd*

LESSON 19

BLM 88: Words to Know: *go, for*
BLM 89: Comprehension: Cause and Effect
BLM 90: Phonemic Awareness: Letter *Dd*
BLM 91: Phonics: Letter *Dd*
BLM 92: Phonemic Awareness: Blend Phonemes

LESSON 20

BLM 93: Words to Know: *is, how, find, this, will, be, go, for*
BLM 94: Comprehension: Sequence of Events
BLM 95: Phonemic Awareness: Blend Phonemes
BLM 96: Phonics: Blend Words
BLM 97: Phonemic Awareness: Letter *Oo*

Unit 5 Growing and Changing

LESSON 21

BLM 98: Words to Know: *make, play*
BLM 99: Comprehension: Understanding Characters
BLM 100: Phonemic Awareness: Letter *Oo*
BLM 101: Phonics: Letter *Oo*
BLM 102: Phonemic Awareness: Letters *Xx, Jj*

LESSON 22

BLM 103: Words to Know: *said, good*
BLM 104: Comprehension: Story Structure
BLM 105: Phonemic Awareness: Letters *Xx, Jj*
BLM 106: Phonics: Letters *Xx, Jj*
BLM 107: Phonemic Awareness: Letter *Ee*

LESSON 23

BLM 108: Words to Know: *she, all*
BLM 109: Comprehension: Sequence of Events
BLM 110: Phonemic Awareness: Letter *Ee*
BLM 111: Phonics: Letter *Ee*
BLM 112: Phonemic Awareness: Letters *Hh, Kk*

LESSON 24

BLM 113: Words to Know: *he, no*
BLM 114: Comprehension: Draw Conclusions
BLM 115: Phonemic Awareness: Letters *Hh, Kk*
BLM 116: Phonics: Letters *Hh, Kk*
BLM 117: Phonemic Awareness: Blend Phonemes

LESSON 25

BLM 118: Words to Know: *make, play, said, good, she, all, he, no*
BLM 119: Comprehension: Text and Graphic Features
BLM 120: Phonemic Awareness: Blend Phonemes
BLM 121: Phonics: Blend Words
BLM 122: Phonemic Awareness: Letter *Uu*

Unit 6 Look at Us

LESSON 26

BLM 123: Words to Know: *do, down*
BLM 124: Comprehension: Cause and Effect
BLM 125: Phonemic Awareness: Letter *Uu*
BLM 126: Phonics: Letter *Uu*
BLM 127: Phonemic Awareness: Letters *Ll, Ww*

LESSON 27

BLM 128: Words to Know: *have, help*
BLM 129: Comprehension: Compare and Contrast
BLM 130: Phonemic Awareness: Letters *Ll, Ww*
BLM 131: Phonics: Letters *Ll, Ww*
BLM 132: Phonemic Awareness: Letters *Vv, Zz*

LESSON 28

BLM 133: Words to Know: *look, out*
BLM 134: Comprehension: Story Structure
BLM 135: Phonemic Awareness: Letters *Vv, Zz*
BLM 136: Phonics: Letters *Vv, Zz*
BLM 137: Phonemic Awareness: Letters *Yy, Qq*

LESSON 29

BLM 138: Words to Know: *off, take*
BLM 139: Comprehension: Main Idea and Details
BLM 140: Phonemic Awareness: Letters *Yy, Qq*
BLM 141: Phonics: Letters *Yy, Qq*
BLM 142: Phonemic Awareness: Words with *a, e, i, o, u*

LESSON 30

BLM 143: Words to Know: *do, down, have, help, look, out, off, take*
BLM 144: Comprehension: Understanding Characters
BLM 145: Phonemic Awareness: Words with *a, e, i, o, u*
BLM 146: Phonics: Blend Words
BLM 147: Phonemic Awareness: Track Syllables

Letters *Aa–Ee*

Aa Bb Cc Dd Ee Ff Gg Hh Ii
Jj Kk Ll Mm Nn Oo Pp Qq Rr
Ss Tt Uu Vv Ww Xx Yy Zz

Aa Bb Cc Dd Ee

Have children circle the small letters *a–e*. Next, have them circle the capital letters in each cloud that match. Then, have children trace the capital and small letters *Aa–Ee* at the bottom of the page.

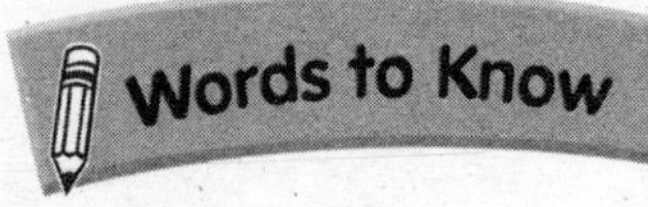

I

1. I 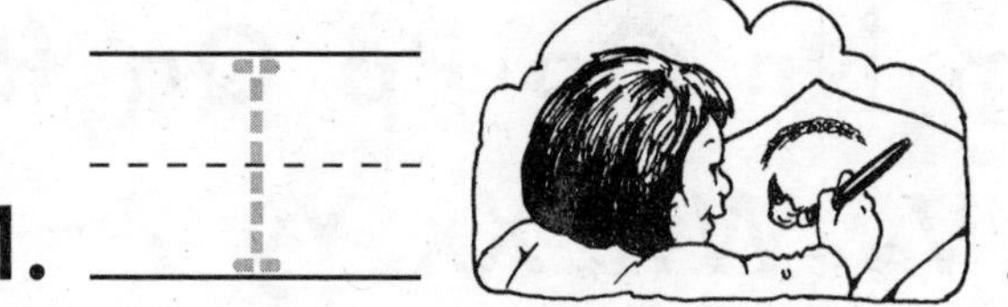 .

2. I 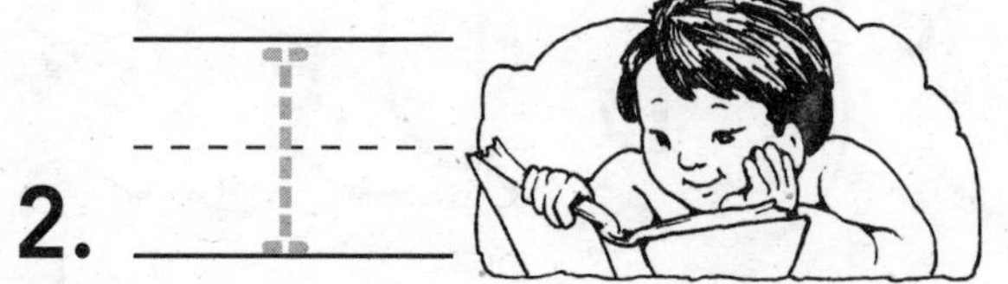 .

3. I 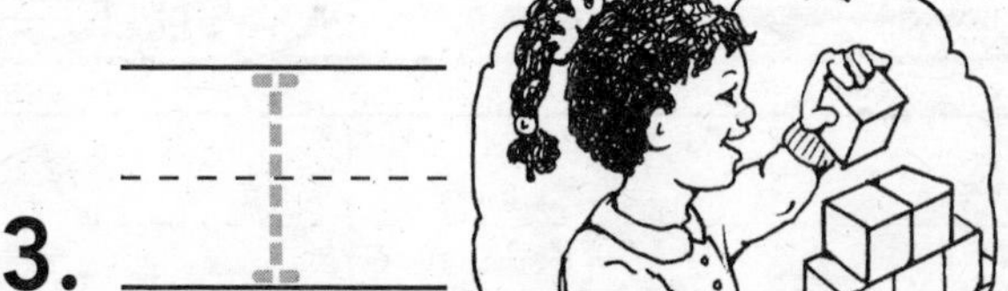 .

4. I  .

Have children say the word *I*. Guide children to complete sentence 1. Have them trace the word *I* and read the sentence aloud. Children complete sentences 2 and 3 on their own. For sentence 4, children draw a picture to complete the sentence. Then have them read the sentence aloud.

Letters *Ff–Jj*

Aa	Bb	Cc	Dd	Ee	Ff	Gg	Hh	Ii	Jj	Kk	Ll	Mm
Nn	Oo	Pp	Qq	Rr	Ss	Tt	Uu	Vv	Ww	Xx	Yy	Zz

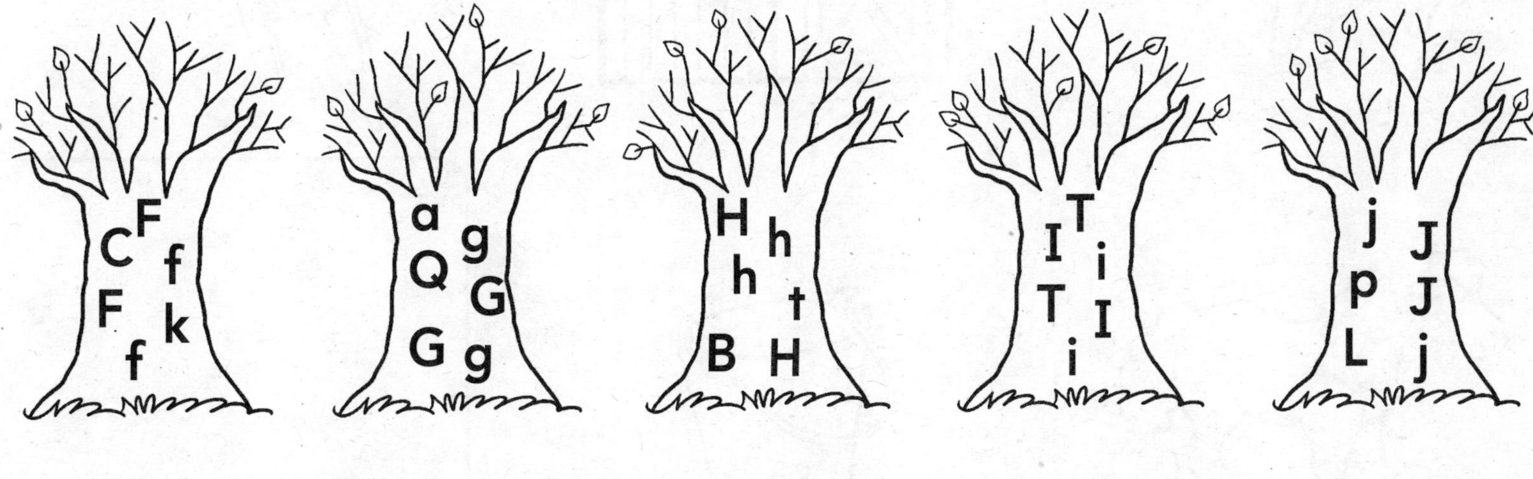

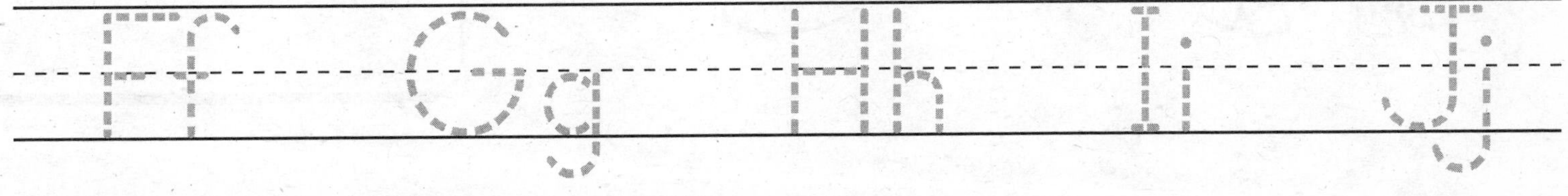

Have children circle the small letters *f–j*. Next, have them circle the matching capital letters on each tree. Then, have children trace the capital and small *Ff–Jj* letters at the bottom of the page.

Main Ideas

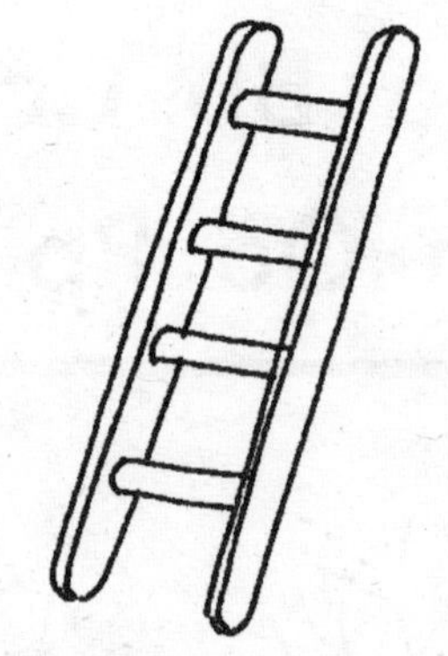

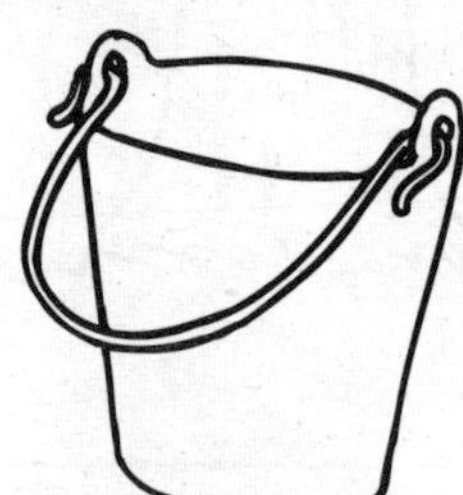

Tell children that one of the pictures shows what the reading was mostly about. The other pictures show some of the details. Have children circle the picture that shows the main idea. Then have children draw a picture in the box that shows another detail from the reading.

Letters *Kk–Oo*

Aa Bb Cc Dd Ee Ff Gg Hh Ii Jj Kk Ll Mm
Nn Oo Pp Qq Rr Ss Tt Uu Vv Ww Xx Yy Zz

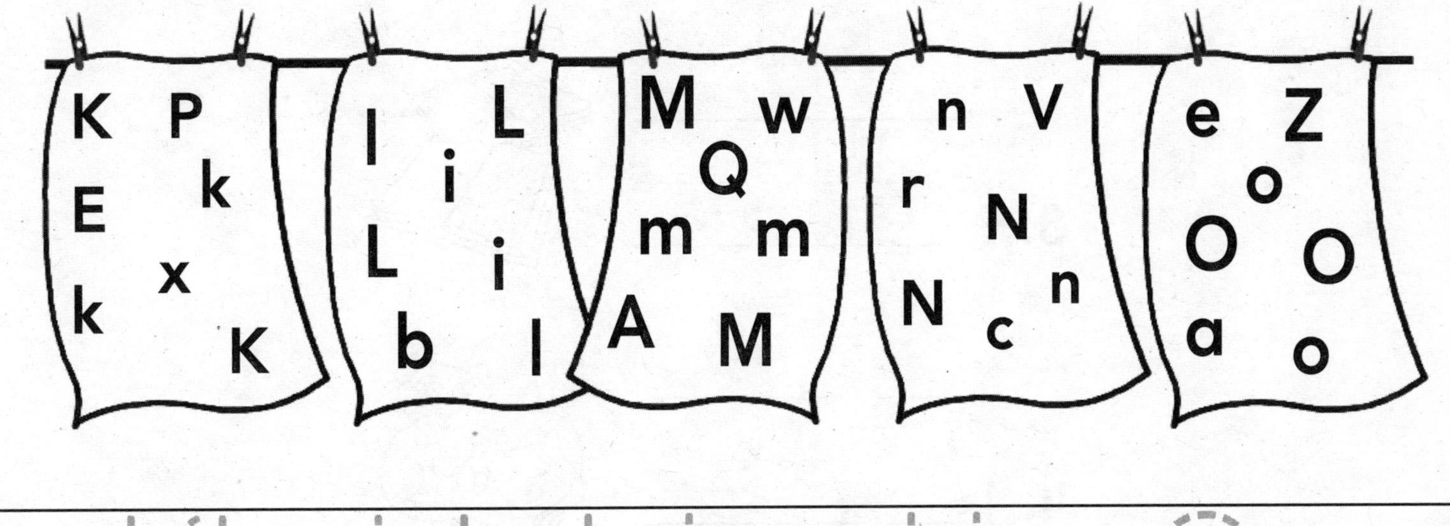

Kk Ll Mm Nn Oo

Have children circle the small letters *k–o*. Next, circle the matching capital letters on each sheet hanging on the clothesline. Then have children trace the capital and small *Kk–Oo* letters at the bottom of the page.

Lesson 2

WORDS TO KNOW

like

1. I like .

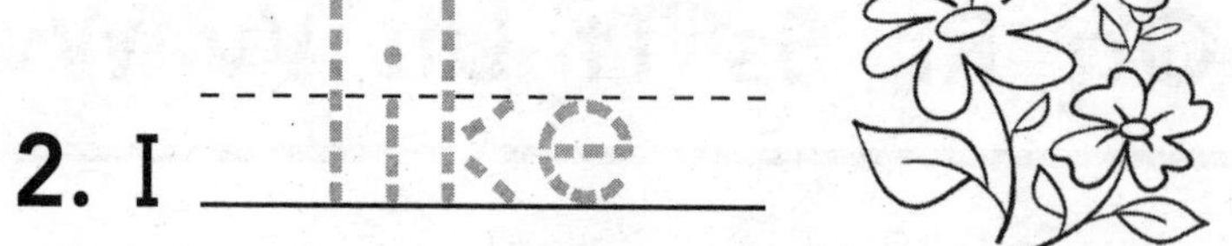

2. I like .

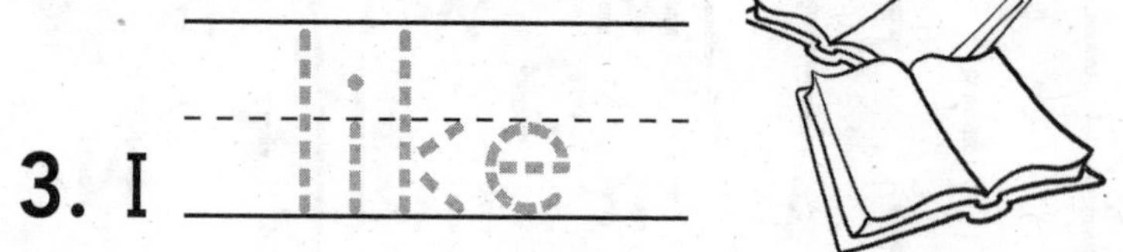

3. I like .

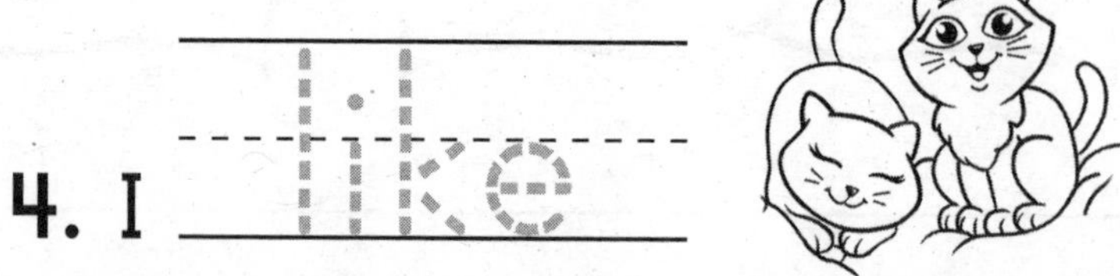

4. I like .

Have children say the word *like*. Guide children to complete sentence 1. Have them trace the word *like* and read the sentence aloud. Children complete sentences 2–4 on their own. Then have them read the sentences aloud.

Comprehension

Understanding Characters

1.

3.

2.

4.

Have children circle the picture in item 1 that shows what the main character likes to do. For item 2, have children draw a face that shows how the main character feels when she rides her bike. For item 3, have children draw a face that shows how the main character feels when her bike is broken. For item 4, have children circle the picture that shows what the main character wants for her birthday.

Letter Names

Letters *Pp–Tt*

Aa Bb Cc Dd Ee Ff Gg Hh Ii Jj Kk Ll Mm
Nn Oo Pp Qq Rr Ss Tt Uu Vv Ww Xx Yy Zz

Have children circle the small letters *p–t*. Next, have them circle the capital letters in each duck that match. Then, have children trace the capital and small letters *Pp–Tt* at the bottom of the page.

Lesson 3

✓ WORDS TO KNOW

the

1. I like the 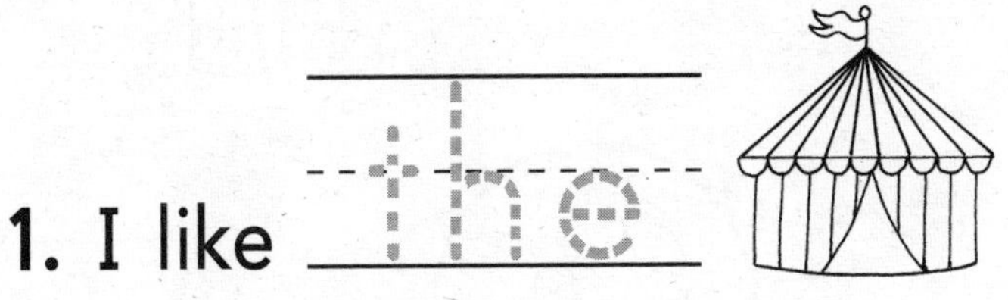 .

3. I like the  .

2. I like the 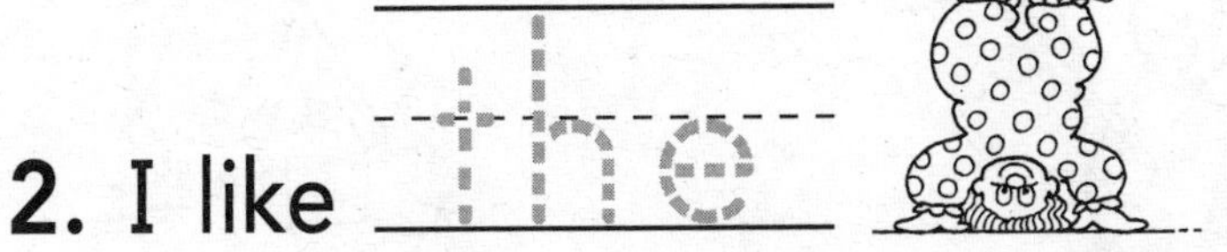 .

4. I like the 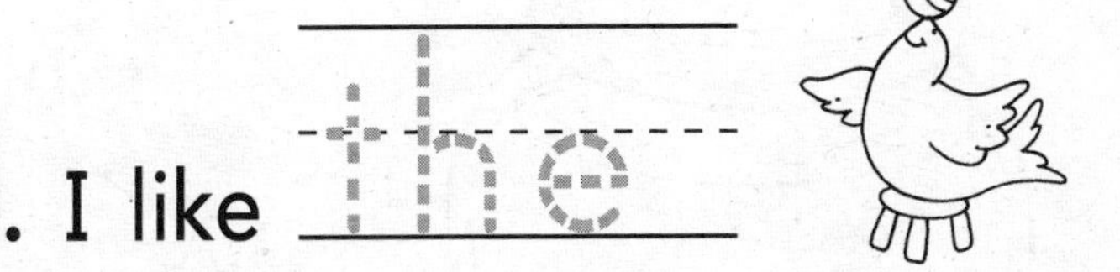 .

Have children say the word *the*. Guide children to complete item 1. Have them trace the word *the* and read the sentence aloud. Children complete items 2, 3, and 4 on their own. Then have them read the sentences aloud.

Comprehension

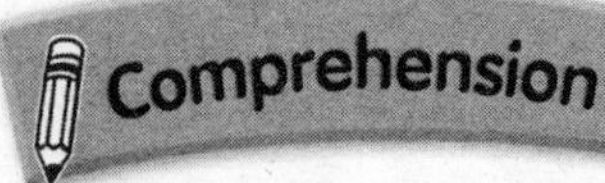

Story Structure

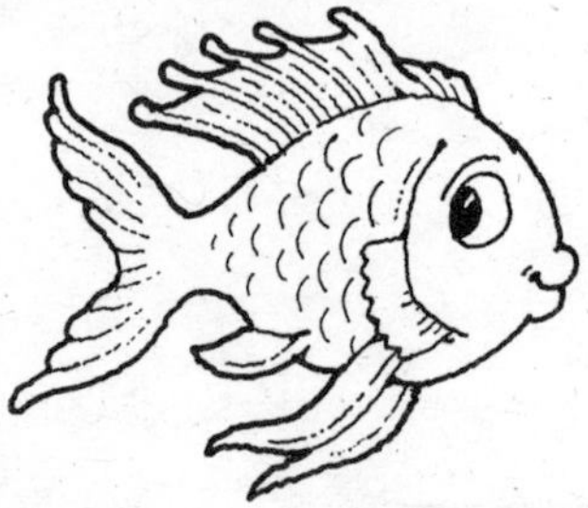

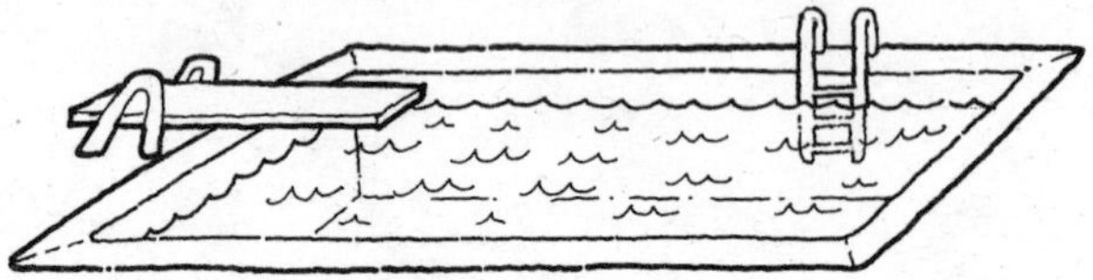

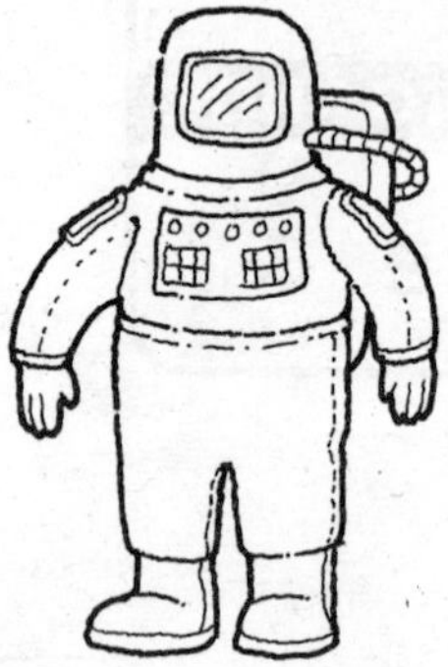

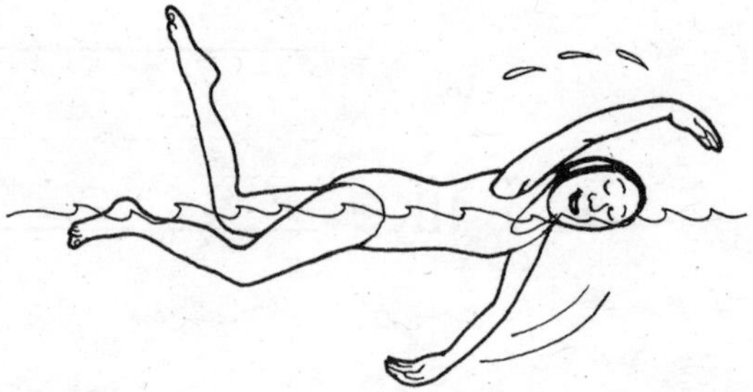

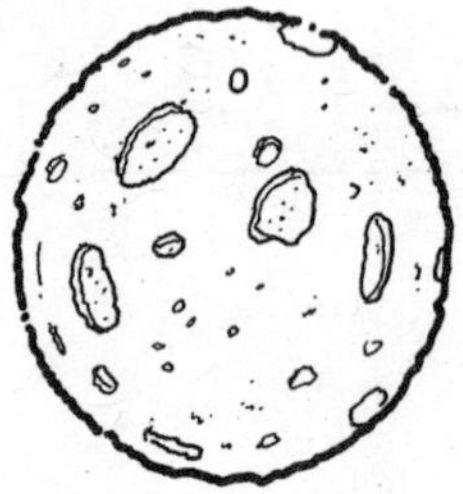

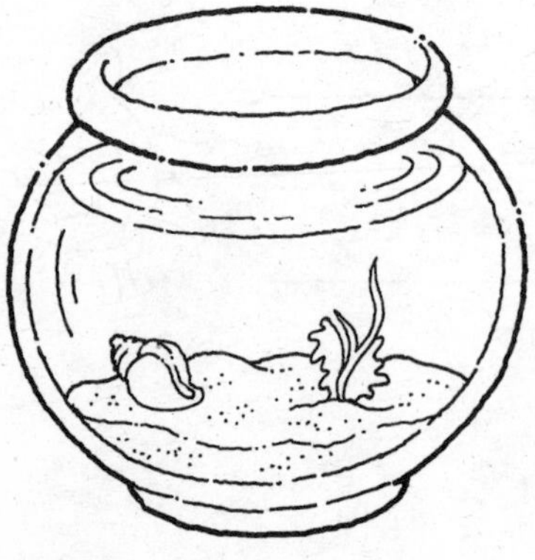

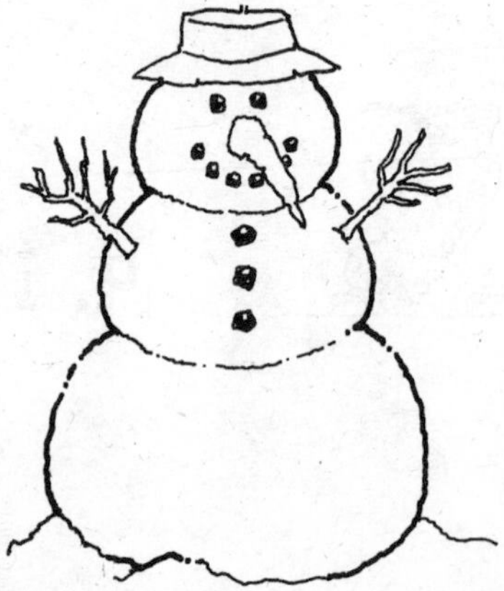

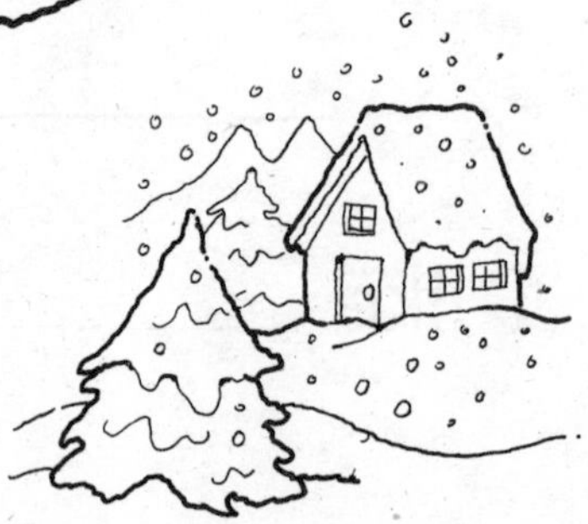

Have children circle pictures that show possible characters in a story. Then have them color the pictures that show places where a story might take place. Tell children to draw a line between each character and the place where its story might happen.

Letters *Uu–Zz*

Aa Bb Cc Dd Ee Ff Gg Hh Ii Jj Kk Ll Mm
Nn Oo Pp Qq Rr Ss Tt Uu Vv Ww Xx Yy Zz

Have children circle the small letters *u–z*. Next, circle the capital letters in each flower that match. Then have children trace the capital and small letters *Uu–Zz* at the bottom of the page.

Letter *Mm*

Have children listen to and point as you name the pictures. Say, *There is a mouse, a mask, a dog, a moon, a book, and a mitten.* Have them color each picture whose name begins with the sound /m/.

Lesson 4

WORDS TO KNOW

and

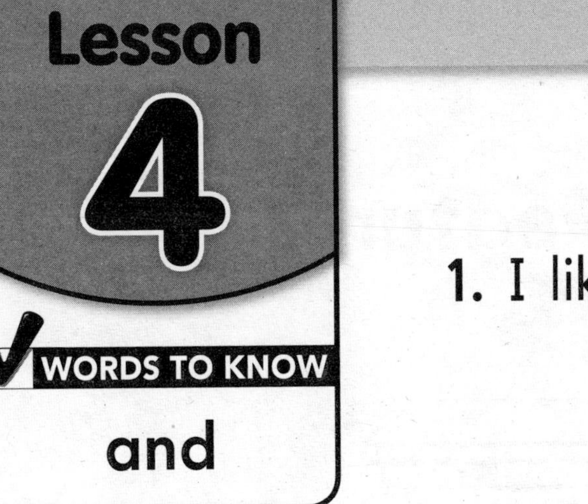

1. I like ______ and ______.
2. I like ______ and ______.
3. I like ______ and ______.
4. I like ______ and ______.

Have children say the word *and*. Complete sentence 1 together. Have them trace the word and read aloud the sentence. Have children complete sentences 2 and 3 on their own. Then have them draw two pictures to complete sentence 4. Then have them read the sentences aloud.

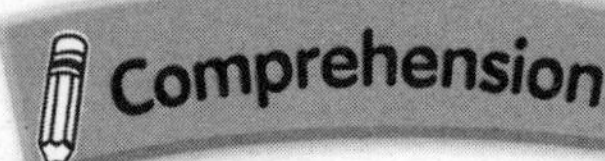

Text and Graphic Features

1. 

2. 

3. 

4. 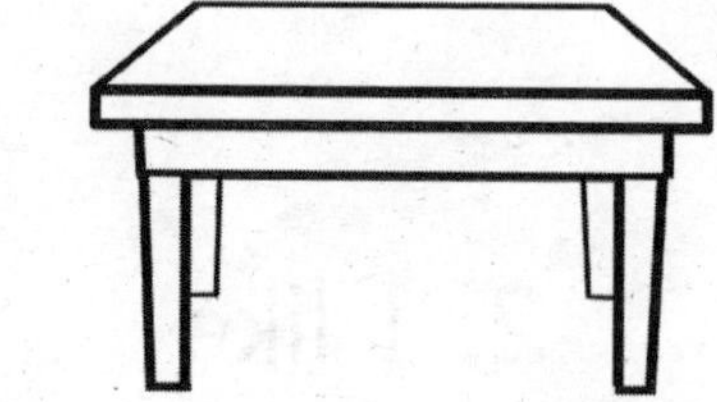

5. 

6. 

Remind children that illustrations can give us more information about what we read. Have children circle the pictures that give more information about Dara's visit to the farm.

Letter *Mm*

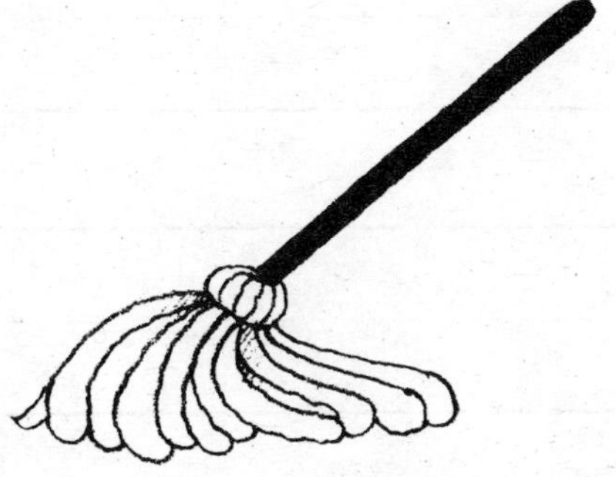

Have children listen and point to the pictures as you name each one: *mop*, *ball*, *mask*, *hat*, *mountain*, *mug*. Have them say the word *mouse* and listen for the beginning sound /m/. Have them color each picture whose name begins the same as *mouse*.

Phonics

Letter *Mm*

Have children point to the mop and say the beginning sound /m/. Have them practice writing capital *M* and small *m*. Name each picture: *mitten*, *moon*, *needle*, *man*, *fish*. Then have children write *Mm* beside the pictures whose names begin with /m/.

Letter *Ss*

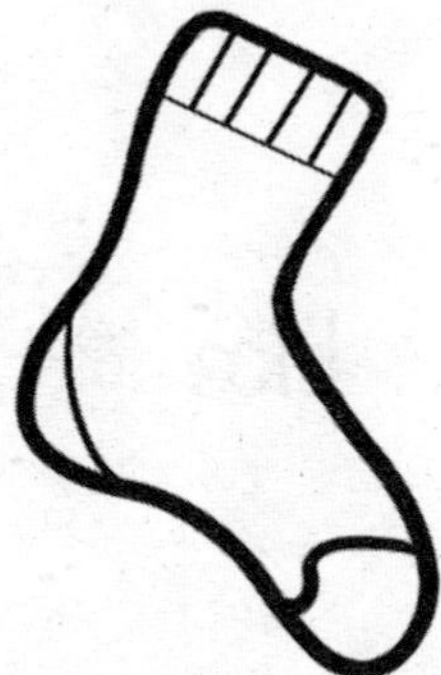

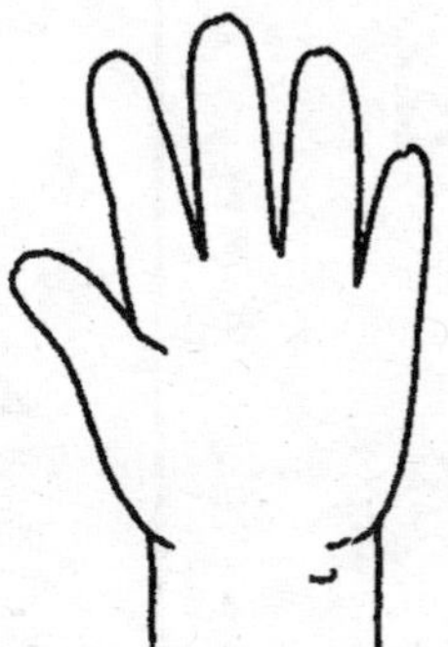

Have children listen to and point as you name the pictures: *sun*, *sock*, *hand*, *soup*, *bike*, *sandwich*. Have them circle each picture whose name begins with the /s/ sound and place an X over any picture that does not begin with the /s/ sound.

Lesson

✓ WORDS TO KNOW

and

I

like

the

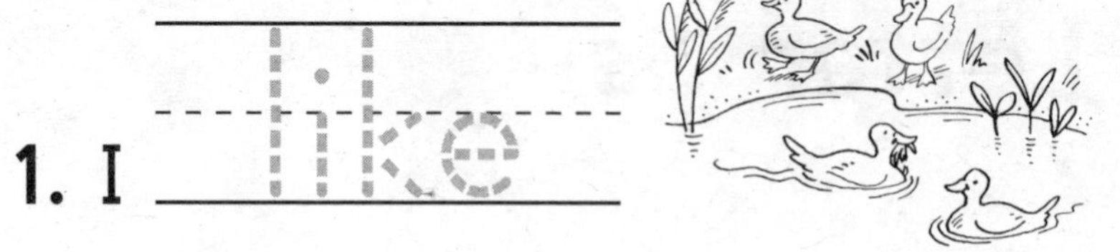

1. I like.

2. I like.

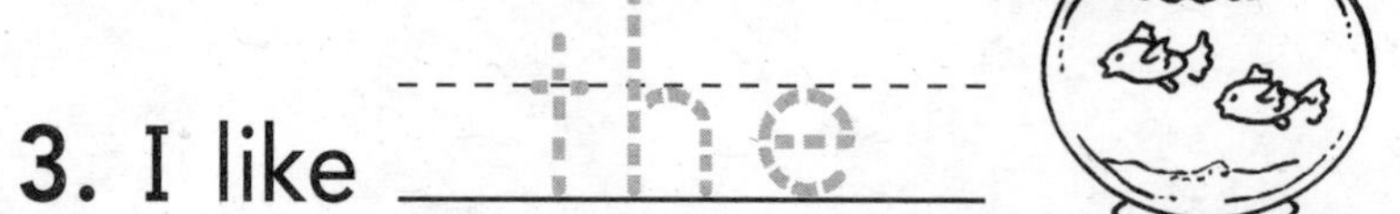

3. I like the.

4. I like the and the.

Have children say the words *and*, *I*, *like*, *the*. Complete sentence 1 with children. Have them trace the word *like* and read the sentence aloud. Repeat the procedure for sentences 2–3. Have children complete sentence 4 with the word *and*, and draw pictures of things they like.

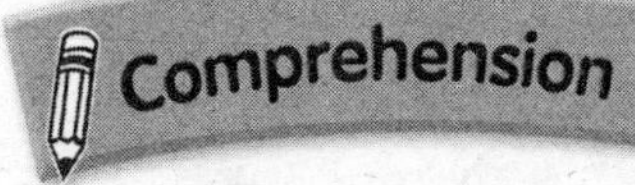

Sequence of Events

Point to the three pictures. Have children describe the action in each picture. Then tell children to write 1, 2, or 3 in the boxes to show what Mom and her family do first, next, and last.

Phonemic Awareness

Letter *Ss*

Have children listen to and point as you name each item in the picture: *seal*, *sun*, *ball*, *sailboat*, *sandals*, *net*, *socks*. Have them say the word *seal* and listen for the beginning sound /s/. Have them color each picture whose name begins with the same sound as *seal*.

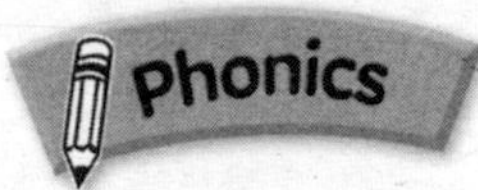

Phonics

Letter *Ss*

1. 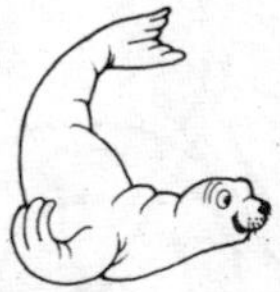 Ss S s

2. 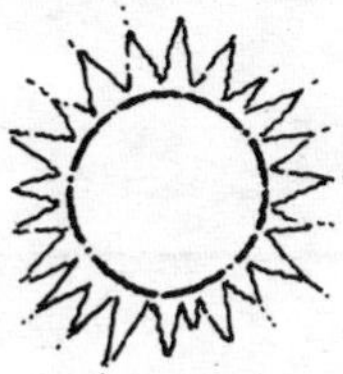

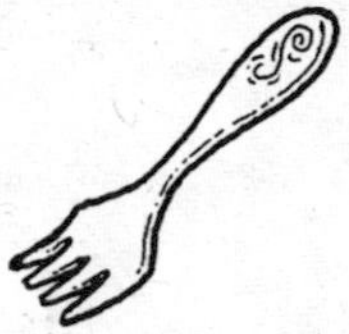

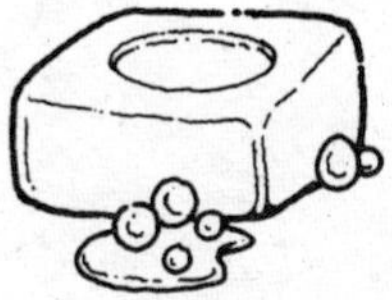

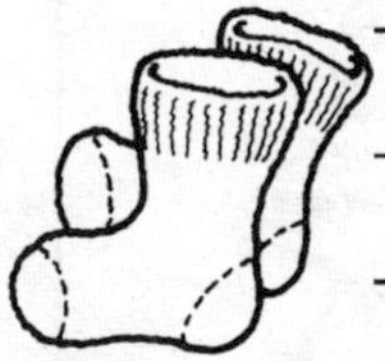

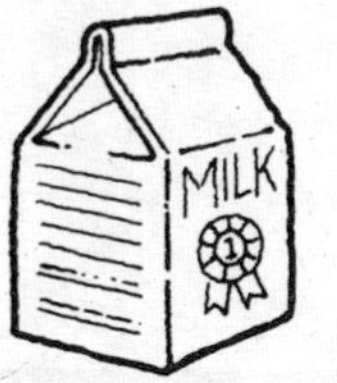

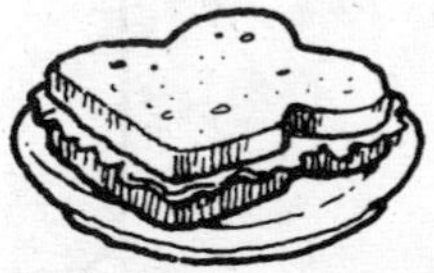

3.

Have children trace the letter *Ss* at the top of the page and practice writing capital *S* and small *s*. Then name the pictures on the page: *sun*, *fork*, *soap*, *socks*, *milk*, *sandwich*. Ask them to write *Ss* beside the pictures whose names begin with /s/. For item 3, have children draw a picture of something that begins with the /s/ sound.

Phonemic Awareness

Letter *Aa*

Have children listen to and point as you name the pictures: *acrobats*, *mop*, *apples*, *bike*, *ant*, *astronaut*. Have them color each picture that has a name that begins with the sound /ă/. Then tell the children to draw another picture that begins with the sound /ă/.

1. I ~~see~~ the .

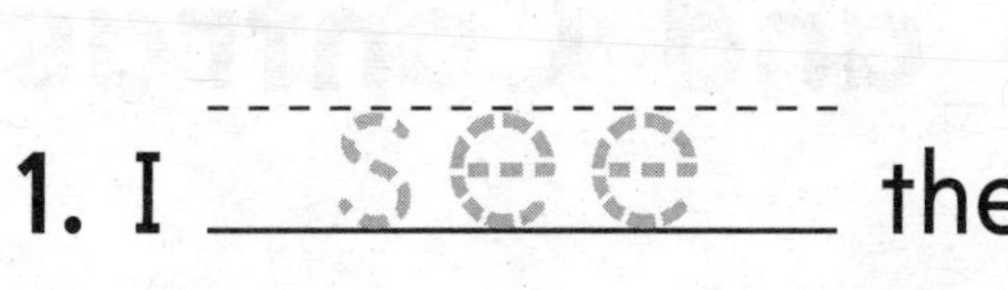

2. I ~~see~~ the .

3. I ~~see~~ the .

4. I ~~see~~ the .

Have children say the word *see*. Do sentence 1 with children. Have them trace the word *see* and read the sentence aloud. Children do 2 and 3 on their own. For sentence 4, children draw a picture to complete the sentence. Then have them read the sentence aloud.

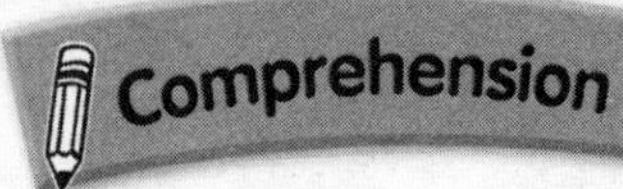

Compare and Contrast

Tell children that a doghouse and your house are both buildings that keep people and pets warm and dry. That's how they are alike. They are also different in many ways. Have children draw a line from each small picture to the correct house. Name the pictures: *bed for a person, dog bed, dishes, dog bowl, dog, girl, window*. Do the first two with children.

Letter *Aa*

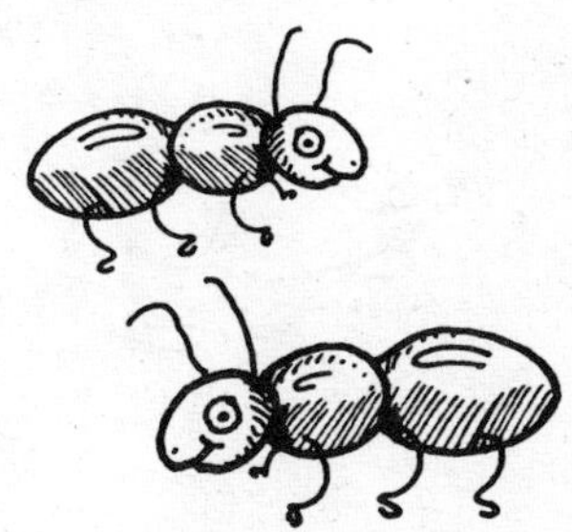

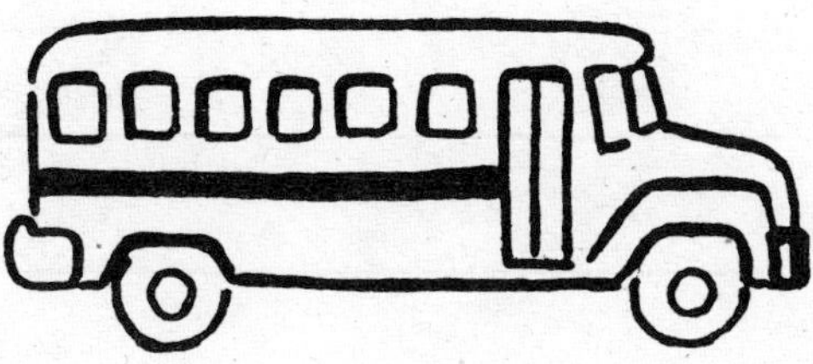

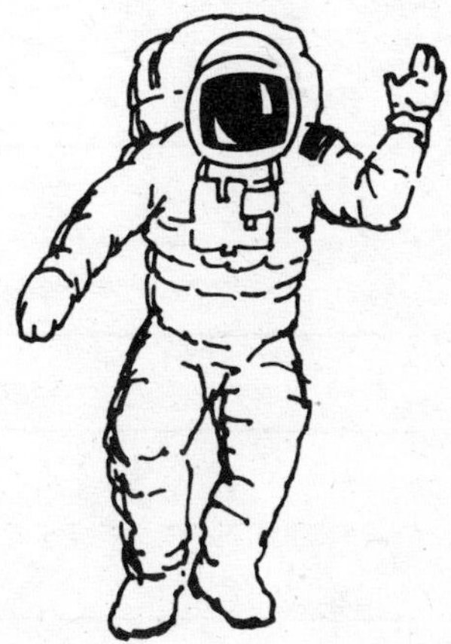

Have children listen and point as you name the pictures: *alligator*, *tent*, *ants*, *bus*, *apple*, *astronaut*. Have them say the word *ax* and listen for the beginning sound /ă/. Have them color each picture whose name begins the same as *ax*.

Phonics Letter *Aa*

Have children point to the apple and say the beginning sound /ă/. Have them practice writing capital *A* and small *a*. Name the remaining pictures: *ax*, *ant*, *mop*, *ambulance*, *dog*. Have children write *Aa* beside the pictures whose names begin with /ă/.

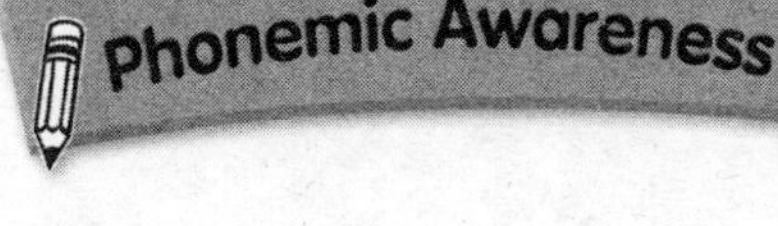

Letter *Tt*

Have children listen to and point as you name the pictures: *tent*, *mouse*, *tooth*, *turtle*, *table*. Have them color each picture whose name begins with the sound /t/. Have them draw one more picture that begins with the sound /t/.

1. We see the .

2. We like .

3. We see and .

4. We like

.

Have children say the word *We*. Do sentence 1 with children. Have them trace the word *We* and read the sentence aloud. Children do 2 and 3 on their own. For sentence 4, children draw a picture to complete the sentence. Then have them read the sentence aloud.

Comprehension

Understanding Characters

1.   

2. 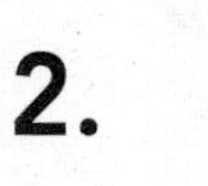   

3.   

4.  likes  .

Have children circle the picture in the first row that shows Tina. Have them circle the picture in the second row that shows how they think Tina feels when she runs. Have children circle the picture in the third row that shows something Tina likes to wear. Then ask, *What does Tina like?* Have children draw a picture to complete sentence 4.

Phonemic Awareness

Letter *Tt*

Have children listen and point as you name the pictures: *table*, *tub*, *mitten*, *ten*, *rocket*, *tack*. Have them say the word *top* and listen for the beginning sound /t/. Tell children to color each picture whose name begins the same as *top*.

Phonics

Letter *Tt*

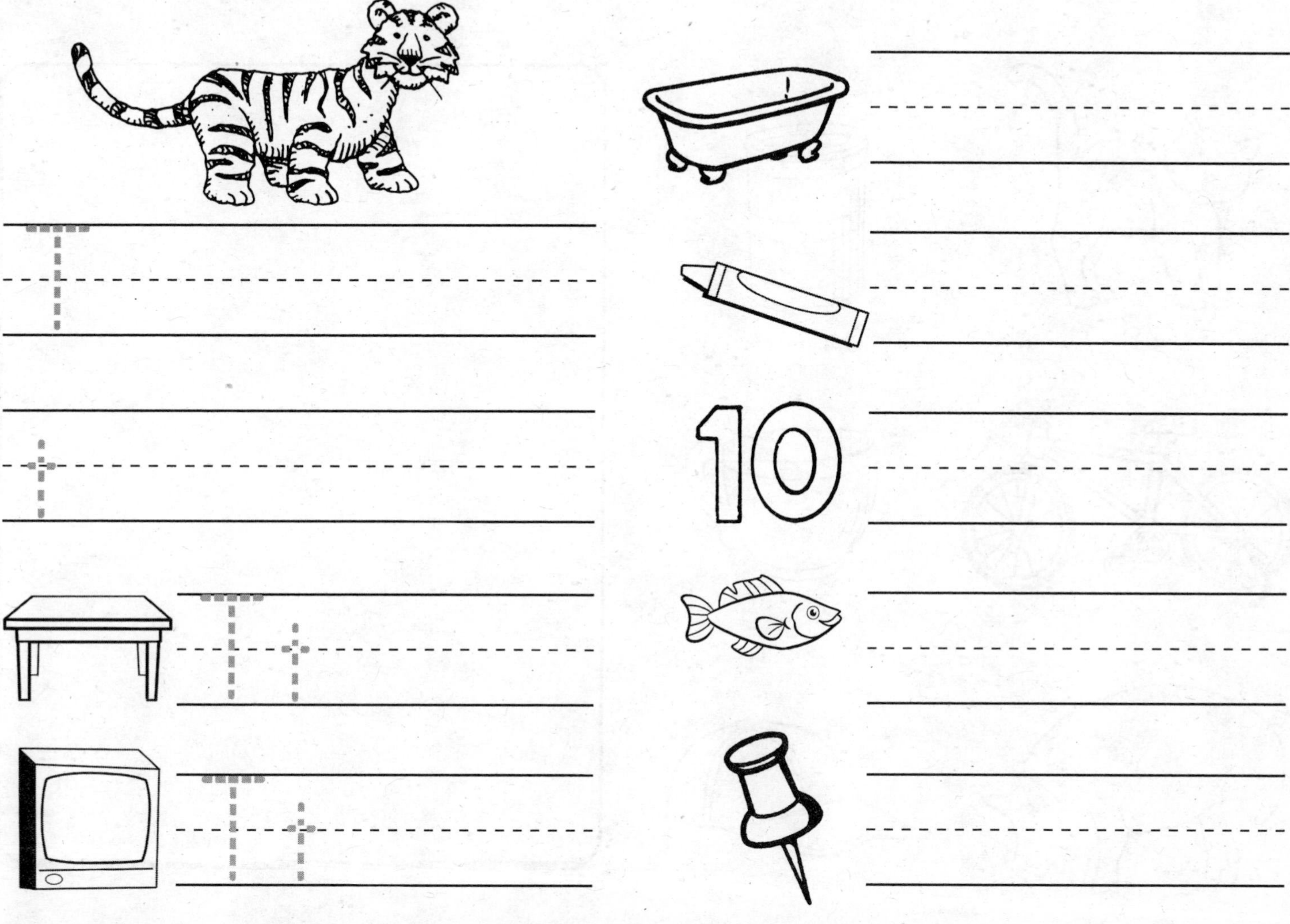

Have children point to the tiger and say the beginning sound /t/. Have them practice writing capital *T* and small *t*. Name the remaining pictures: *table*, *television*, *tub*, *crayon*, *ten*, *fish*, *tack*. Have children write *Tt* beside the pictures whose names begin with /t/.

Phonemic Awareness

Letter Cc

Have children listen to and point as you name the pictures: *cat*, *can*, *bike*, *cup*, *pig*, *cap*. Have them color each picture whose name begins with the sound /k/. Have them draw one more picture that begins with the sound /k/.

1. I see a 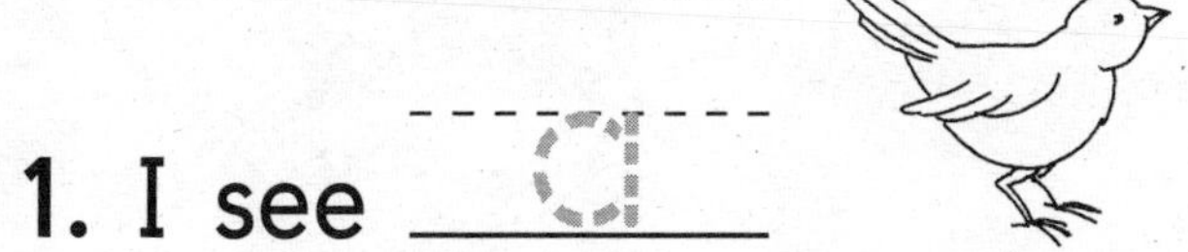 .

2. I see a 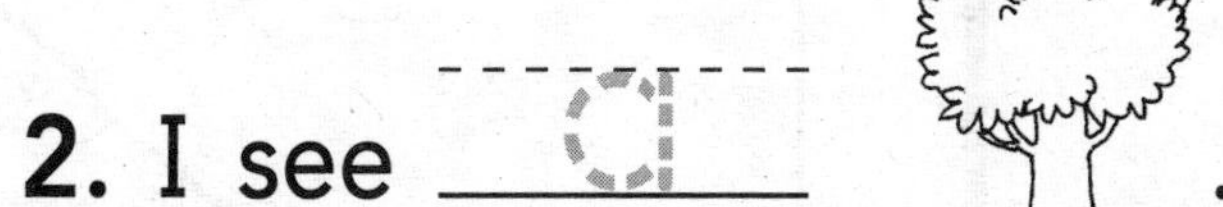 .

3. I see a 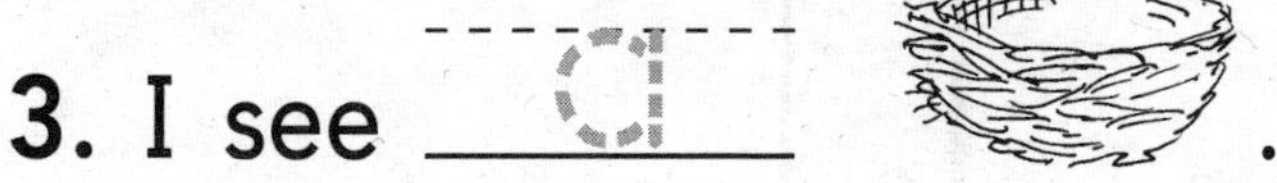 .

4. I see a 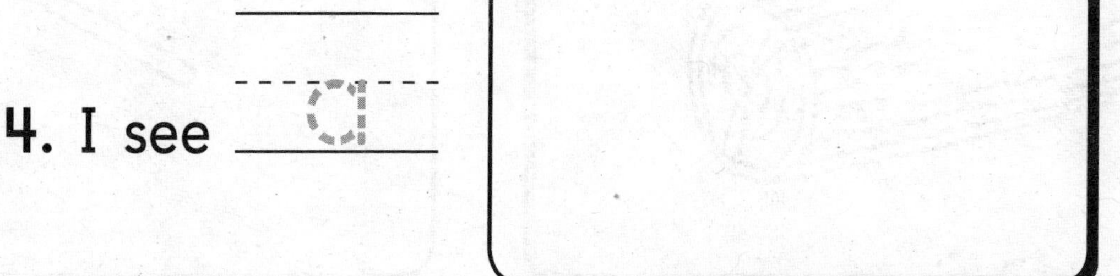 .

Have children say the word *a*. Do sentence 1 with children. Have them trace the word *a* and read the sentence aloud. Children do 2 and 3 on their own. For sentence 4, children draw a picture to complete the sentence. Then have them read the sentence aloud.

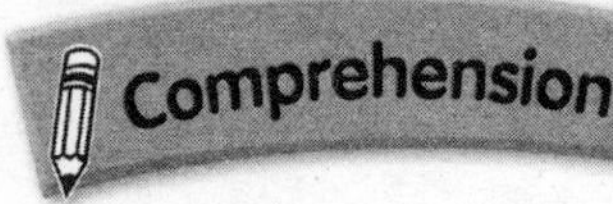

Details

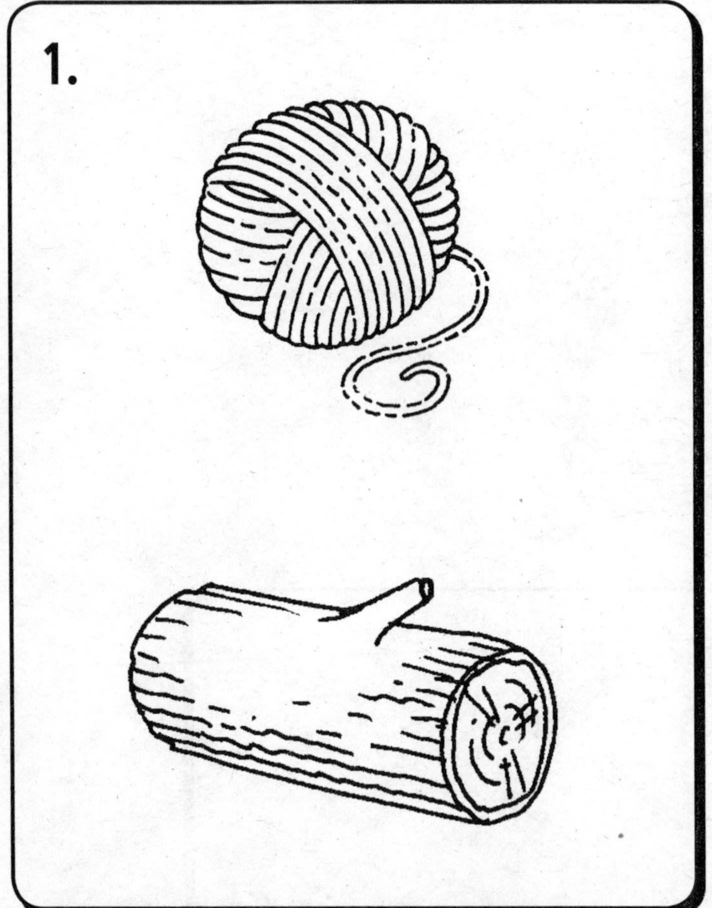

Have children listen to the questions about the story and circle the correct answer. For item 1, ask, *What did Jessie's uncle use to make the table?* For item 2, ask, *Which tool does a carpenter use?*

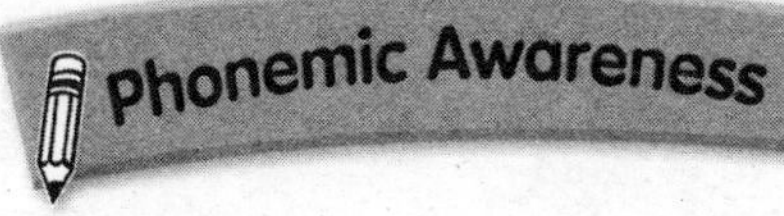

Letter Cc

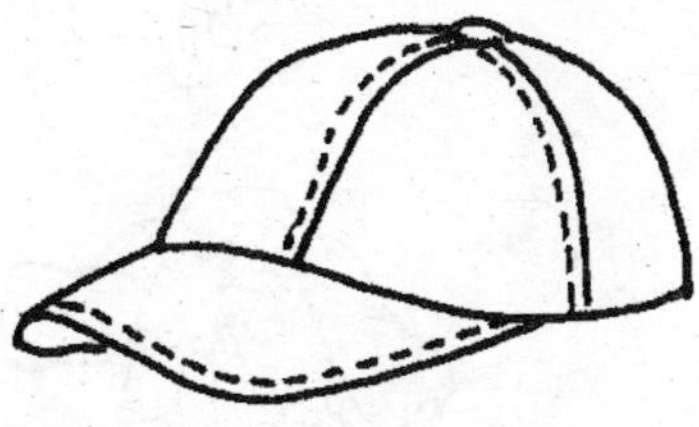

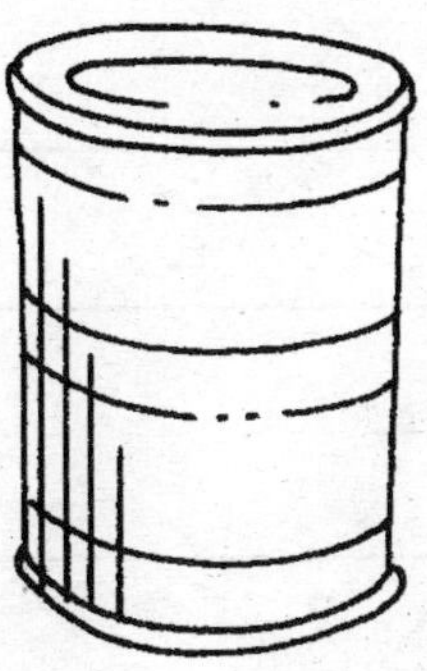

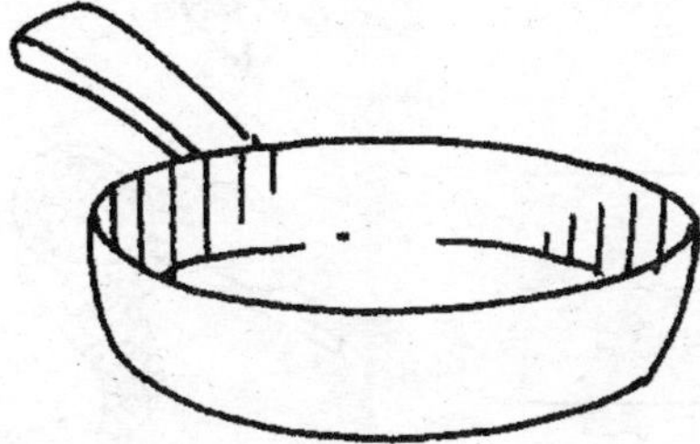

Have children listen to and point as you name the pictures: *sandwich*, *cap*, *cat*, *can*, *pan*, *comb*. Have them say the word *car* and listen for the beginning sound /k/. Tell them to circle each picture whose name begins the same as *car*.

Phonics Letter Cc

Have children point to the cat and say the word *cat* emphasizing the beginning sound /k/. Have them practice writing a capital *C* and a small *c*. Then point to and name the rest of the pictures on the page: *bus*, *coat*, *carrots*, *net*, *car*. Tell children to write *Cc* beside the pictures whose names being with /k/.

Letter *Pp*

Have children listen to and point as you name the pictures: *pan, ball, puppy, pencil, pig, cow, horse, pie.* Have children circle the objects whose names begin with the /p/ sound.

Lesson 9

✓ WORDS TO KNOW

to

1. I like to 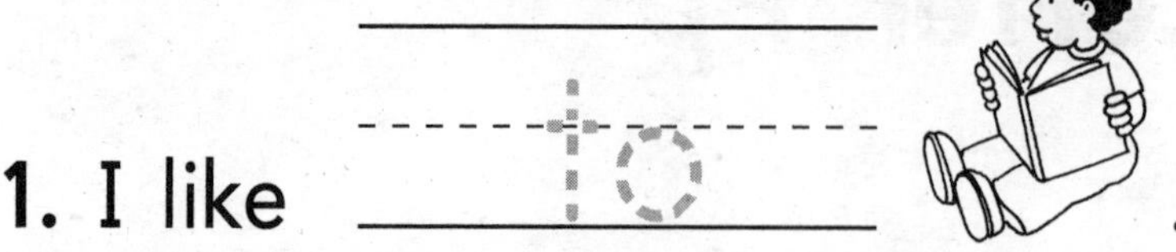.

2. I like to 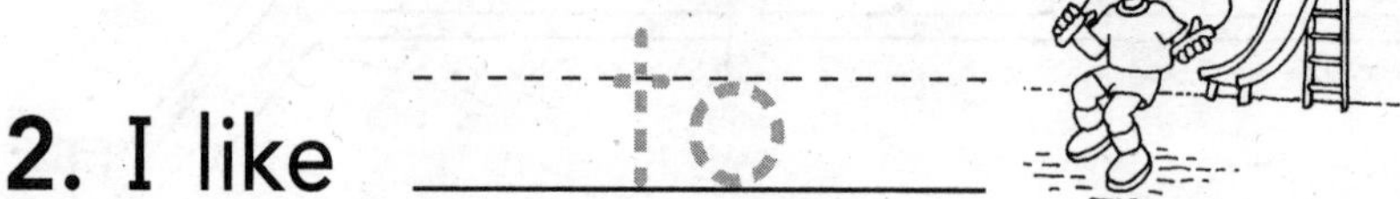.

3. I like to 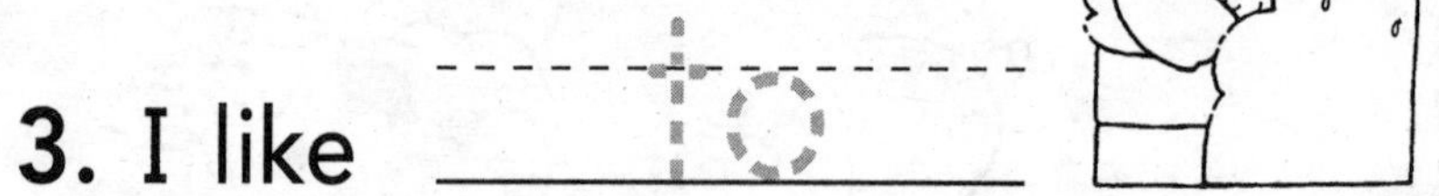.

4. I like to .

Have children say the word *to*. Do sentence 1 with children. Have them trace the word *to* and read the sentence aloud. Children do sentences 2 and 3 on their own. For sentence 4, children draw a picture to complete the sentence. Then have them read the sentence aloud.

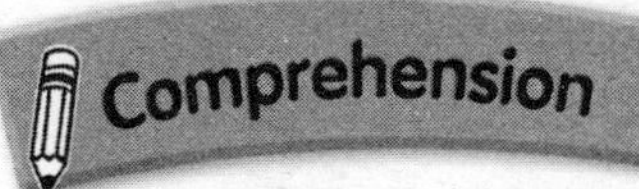

Text and Graphic Features

Have children tell what they know about the clown's shoes from the story. Then discuss the clown's shoes in the picture. Have children circle the parts in the picture that give them new information about the clown's shoes.

Phonemic Awareness

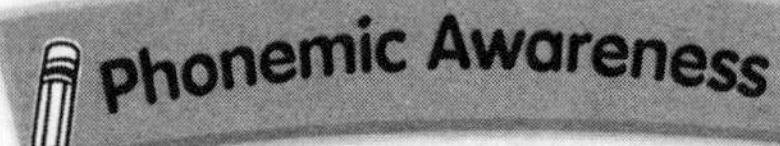

Letter *Pp*

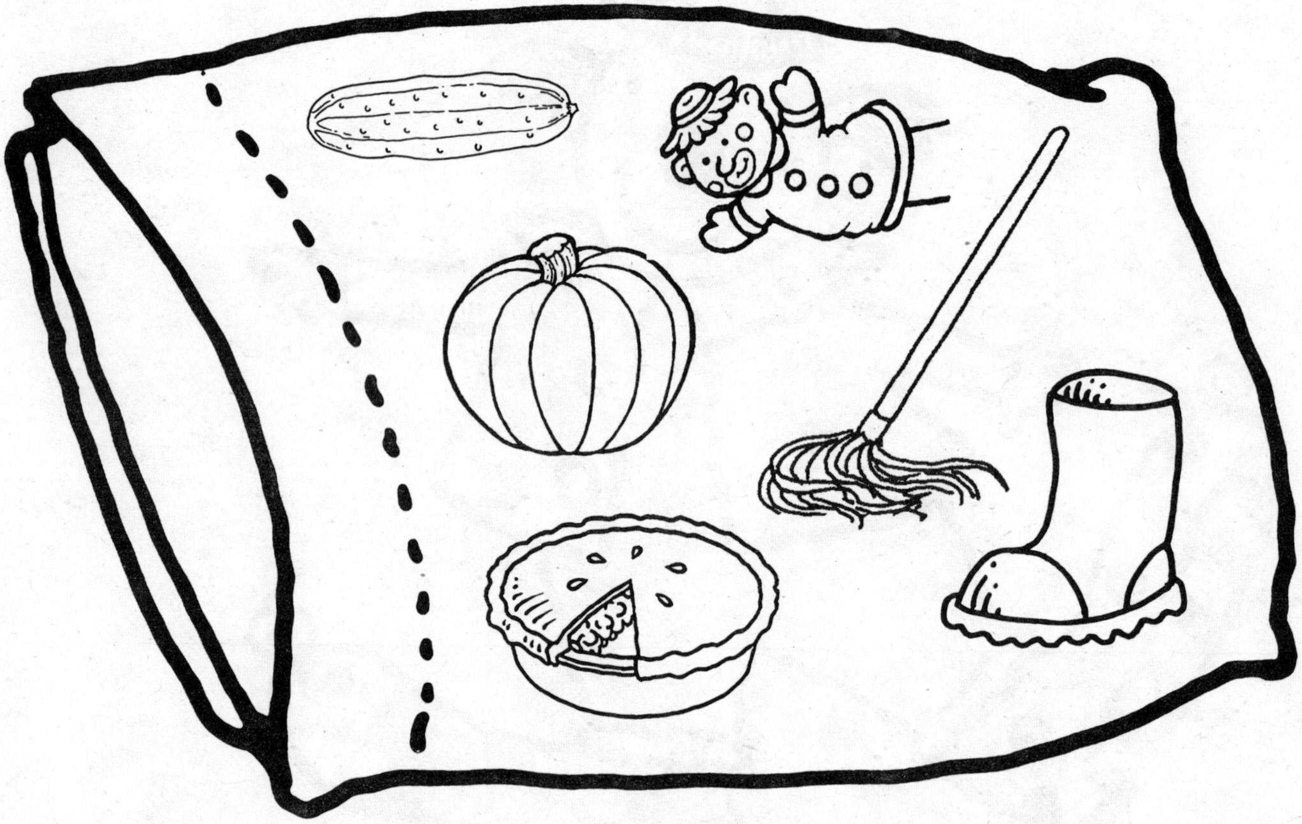

Have children listen to and point as you name the pictures: *puppet, pie, pickle, boot, pumpkin, mop*. Have them say the word *pillow* and listen for the beginning sound /p/. Have them circle and color each picture whose name begins the same as *pillow*.

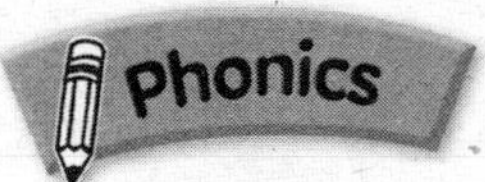

Letter *Pp*

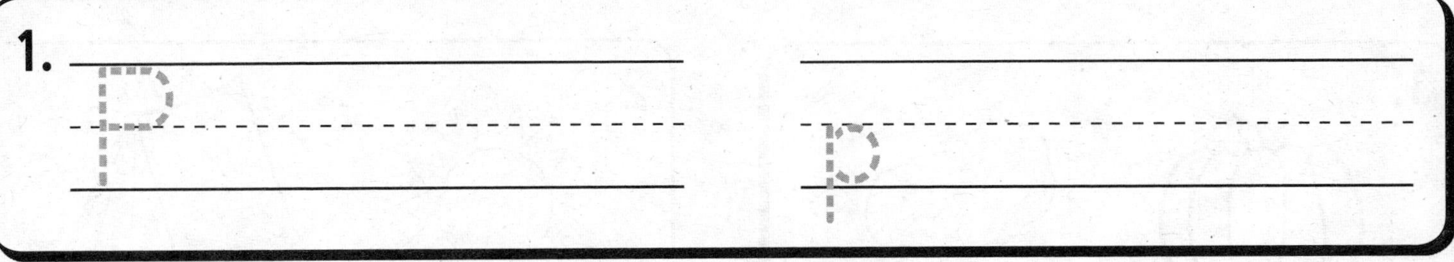

For item 1, have children practice writing capital *P* and small *p*. For item 2, say the picture names: *purse*, *paint*, *pie*, *fork*, *pail*. Have children write *Pp* beside the pictures whose names begin with the /p/ sound. For item 3, have children draw pictures of two more things whose names begin with the /p/ sound.

Phonemic Awareness

Letters *Mm*, *Ss*, *Aa*, *Tt*, *Cc*, *Pp*

1.

2.

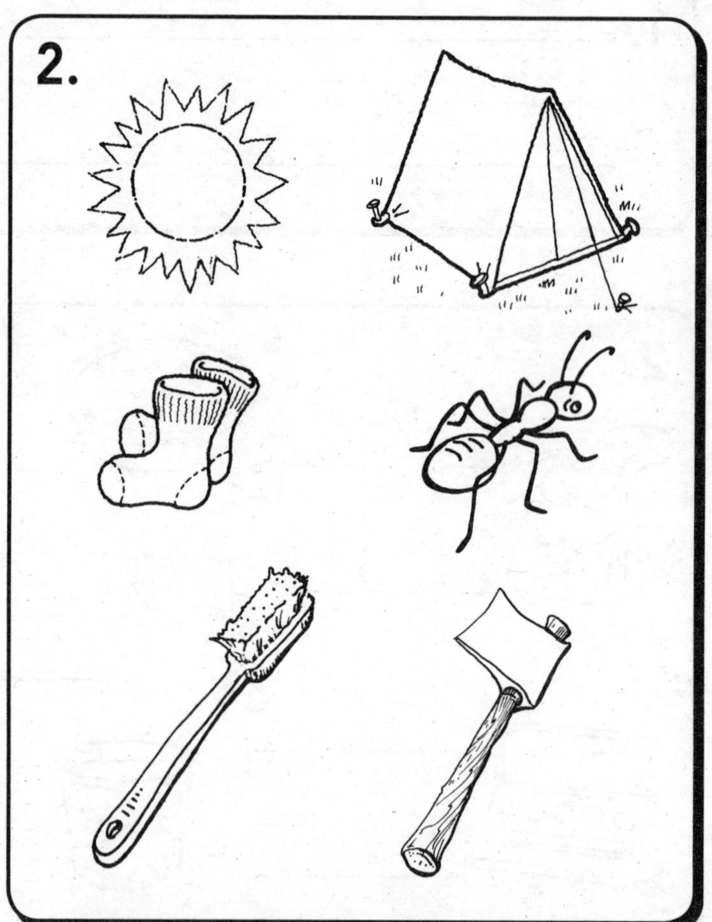

Name each picture in item 1: *pumpkin*, *potato*, *coat*, *camera*, *mop*, *mouse*. Have children draw a line from the *pumpkin* to another picture that starts with the same sound. Repeat for *coat* and *mop*. For item 2, say the picture names: *socks*, *sun*, *toothbrush*, *tent*, *ax*, *ant*. Have children draw lines to match pictures whose names begin with the same sound.

Lesson 10

WORDS TO KNOW

see

we

a

to

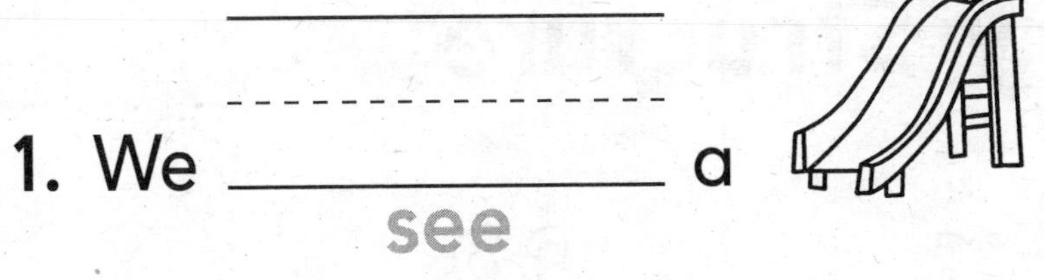

1. We ______ a [slide] .

see
to

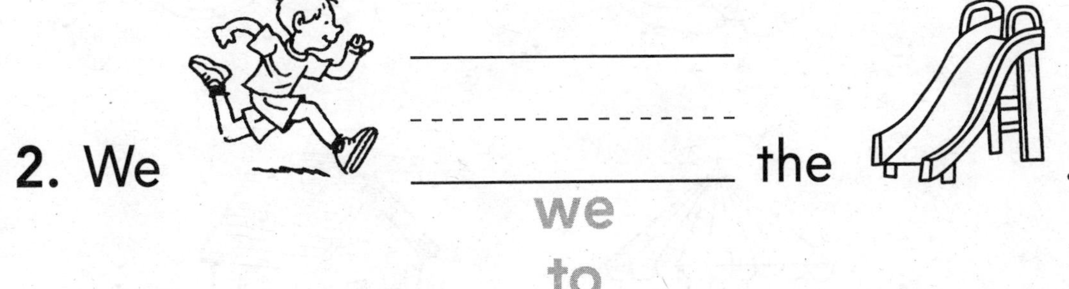

2. We [run] ______ the [slide] .

we
to

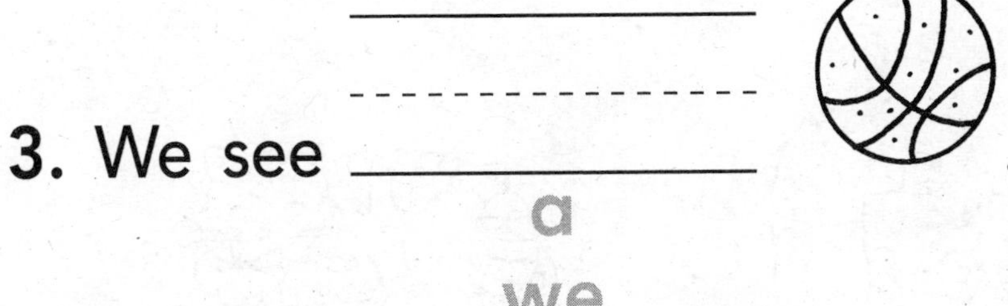

3. We see ______ [ball] .

a
we

Read sentence 1 with each of the word choices. Have children point to and write the correct word. Then have them read the sentence aloud. Continue with sentences 2 and 3.

Comprehension

Story Structure

1.  

2. 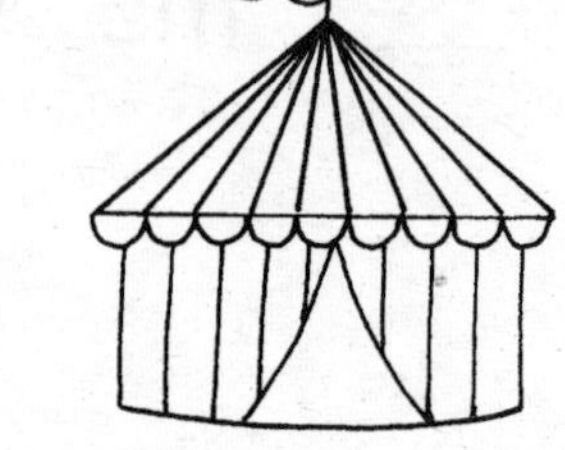 

3.  

Point to the pictures in each item and name them. Tell children to circle the picture in item 1 that shows who the story is about. Tell children to circle the picture in item 2 that shows where the story takes place. Tell children to circle the picture in item 3 that shows an important event from the story.

Phonemic Awareness

Letters *Mm*, *Ss*, *Aa*, *Tt*, *Cc*, *Pp*

Name the pictures in the left column one at a time: *mouse*, *sun*, *apple*, *table*, *cat*, *pie*. Have children listen to the beginning sound in each word and draw a line to the picture on the right whose name begins with the same sound: *ax*, *monkey*, *candle*, *sandwich*, *pig*, *tent*.

Phonics

Letters *Mm*, *Ss*, *Aa*, *Tt*, *Cc*, *Pp*

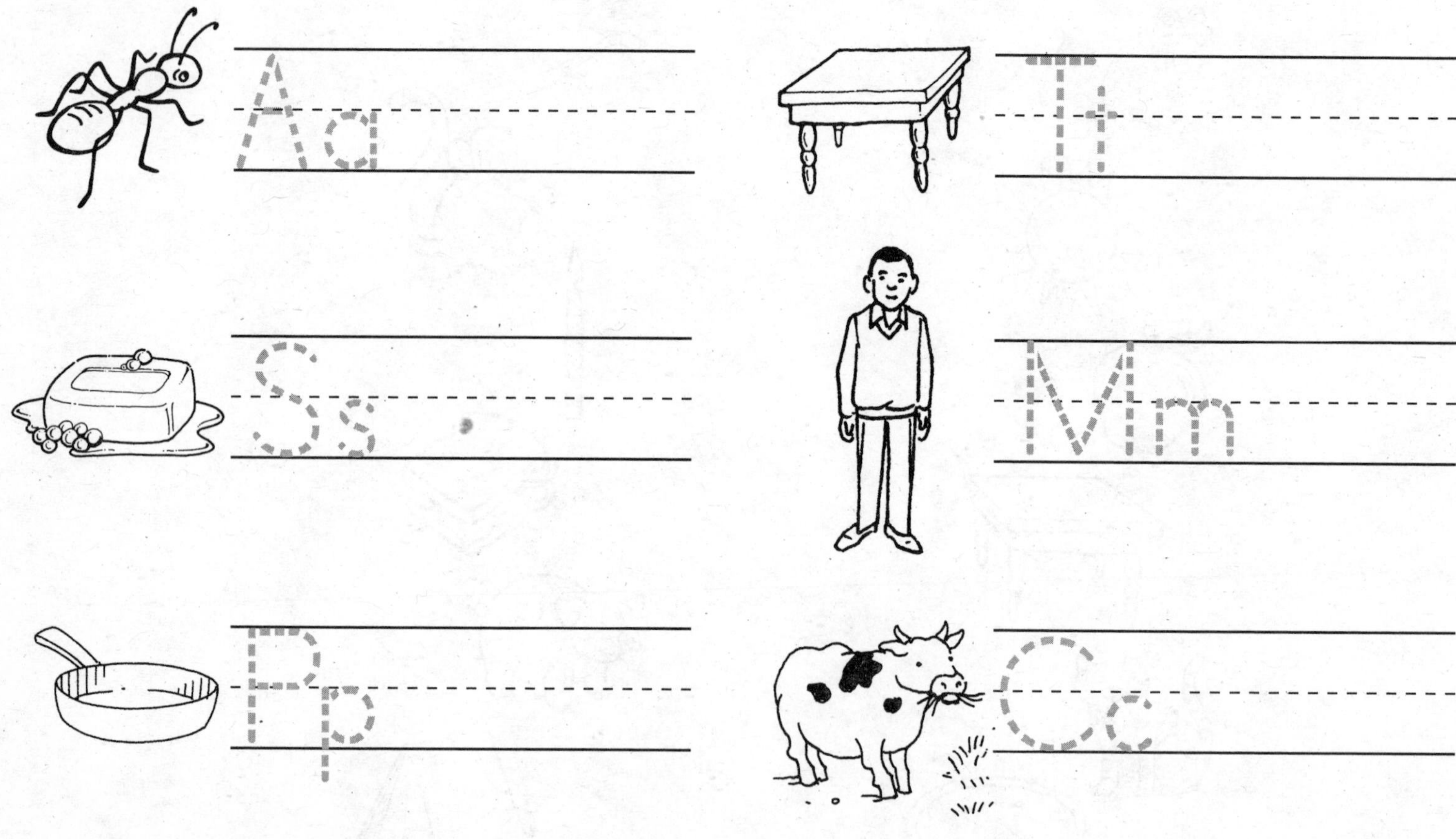

Tell children to listen for the beginning sounds as you name the pictures in each column: *ant*, *soap*, *pan*, *table*, *man*, *cow*. Have children practice writing the letters *Mm*, *Ss*, *Aa*, *Tt*, *Cc*, or *Pp* beside each picture to tell the letter that stands for the sound they hear.

Phonemic Awareness

Letter *Aa*

Have children say the word *cat* and listen for the middle sound /ă/. Then have them listen to and point as you name the pictures one at a time: *man*, *van*, *bus*, *map*, *bat*, *duck*. Have them circle each picture whose name has the same middle sound as *cat*. Finally, invite children to draw their own picture of something whose name has the middle sound /a/.

Lesson

11

✓ WORDS TO KNOW

come

me

1. The [dog] can come.

2. Can the [dog] come to me ?

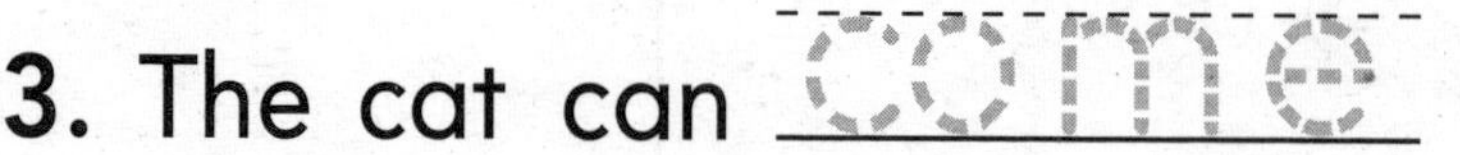

3. The cat can come .

4. The cat can come to me .

Have children say *come* and *me*. Have them trace the word *come* in sentence 1. Read the sentence aloud together. Repeat for sentences 2–4.

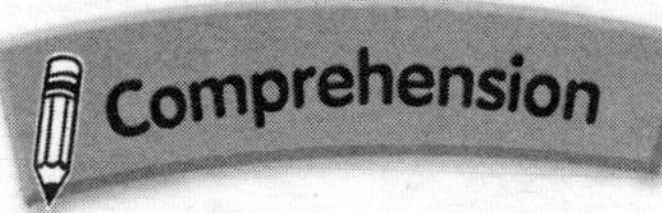

Compare and Contrast

Tell children that the snowmen are alike in some ways and different in other ways. Have children draw a circle around the things that are alike. Have children draw an X over the things that are different.

Letter *Aa*

Have children listen and point as you name the pictures: *van*, *hat*, *bat*, *mat*, *girl*, *dog*. Have them say the word *cat* and listen for the middle sound /ă/. Tell them to circle each picture whose name has the same middle sound as *cat*.

Phonics

Letter *Aa*

Have children point to the astronaut and say the beginning sound /ă/. Have them practice writing capital *A* and small *a*. Then name the pictures: *pan*, *map*, *fish*, *cat*, *dog*. Tell children to write *Aa* beside the pictures whose names have the /ă/ sound in the middle.

Letter *Nn*

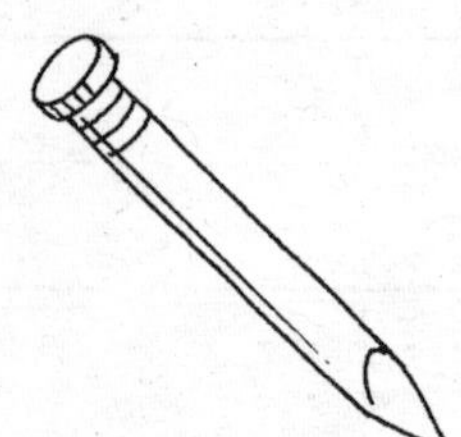

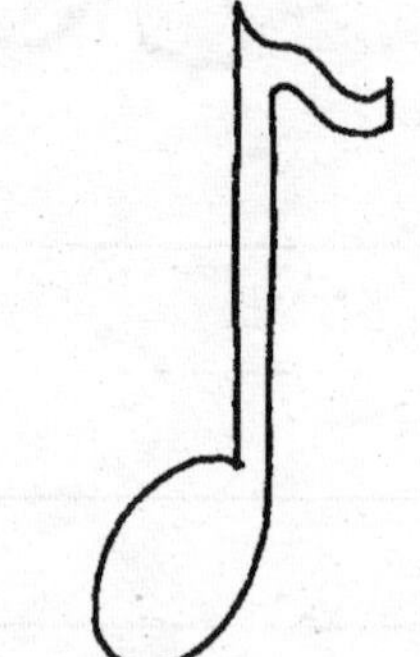

Have children listen and point as you name the pictures: *nest*, *nuts*, *brush*, *nail*, *fish*, *note*. Have them say the word *nap* and listen for the beginning sound /n/. Have them color each picture whose name begins the same as *nap*.

1. I see my .

2. I like my .

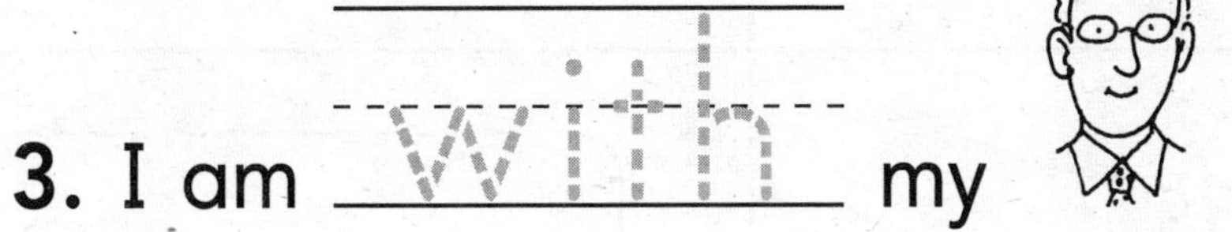

3. I am with my .

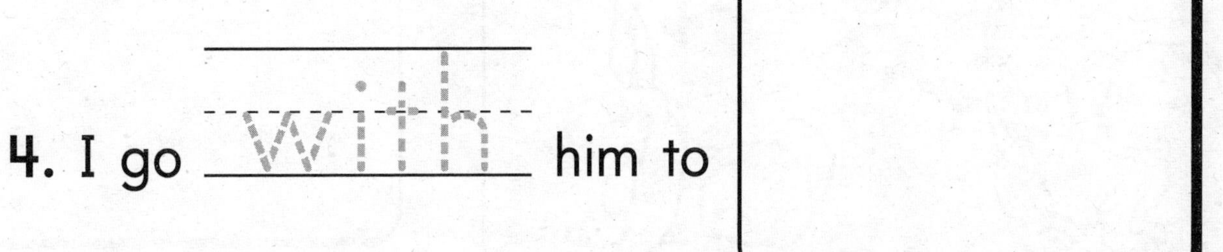

4. I go with him to .

Have children say the words *my* and *with*. Do sentence 1 with children. Have them trace the word *my* and read the sentence aloud. Repeat the procedure for sentence 2. Read sentence 3 with children: *I am with my Dad*. Have children trace the word *with* and read the sentence aloud. Then read sentence 4 to children. Have them draw a picture to complete the sentence.

Comprehension Draw Conclusions

For items 1–3, have children circle the picture that correctly answers the following questions.
For item 4, have children draw a picture of Maggie.

1. *How does Theo feel when he sees Maggie for the first time?*
2. *Which object could be in Theo's backpack?*
3. *Which picture shows a clue to tell us that Maggie is a puppy?*

Letter *Nn*

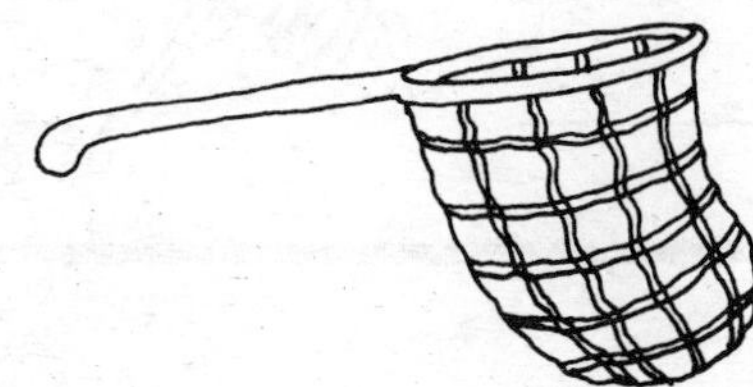

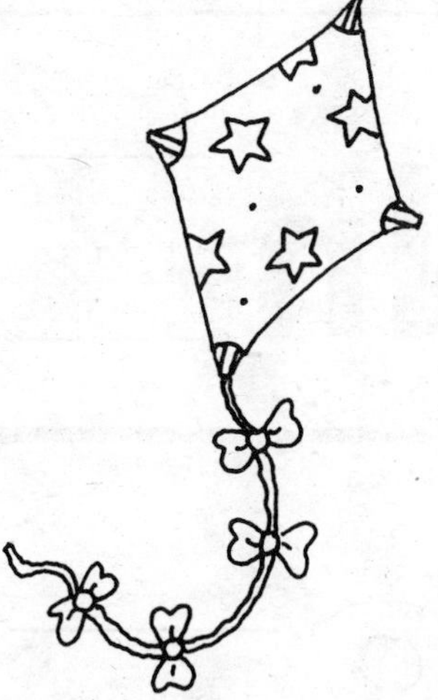

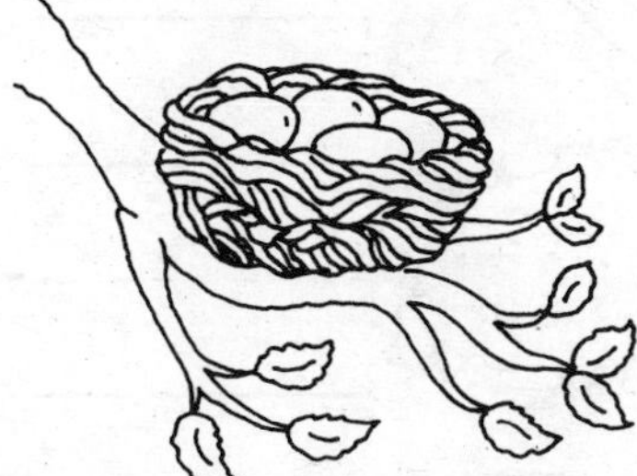

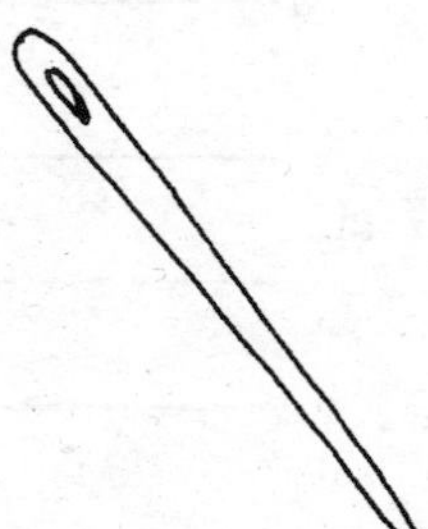

Have children listen and point to each picture as you name it: *notebook*, *net*, *kite*, *soap*, *nest*, *needle*. Have them circle each picture whose name begins with the /n/ sound and place an X over any picture that does not begin with the /n/ sound.

Letter *Nn*

1.

Nn N n

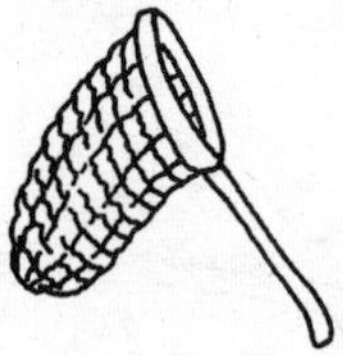

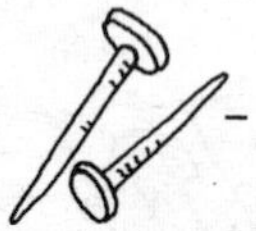

2.

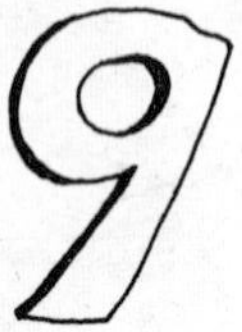

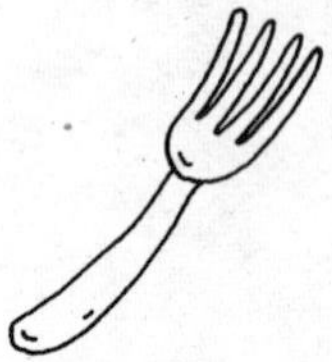

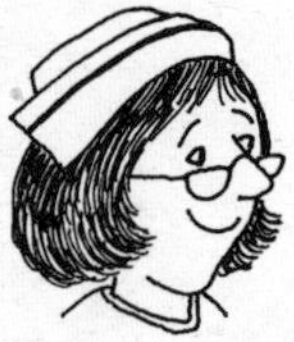

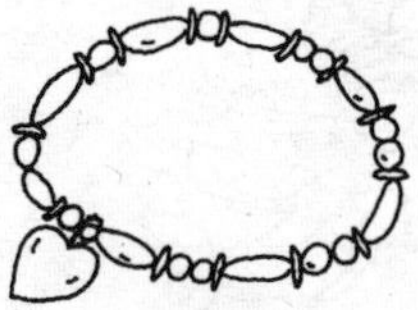

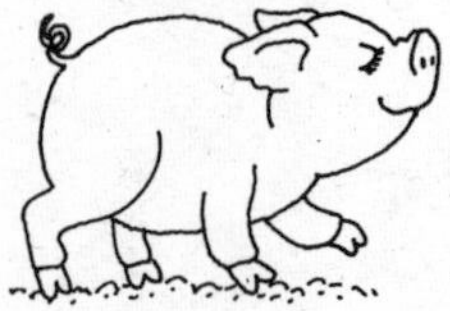

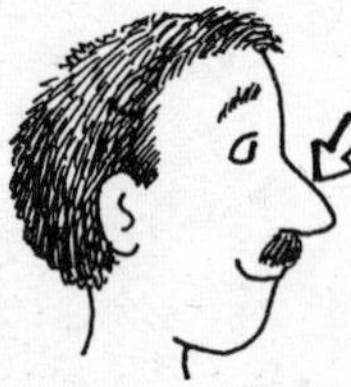

3.

For item 1, say the picture names: *net*, *nails*. Have children practice writing capital and small *N* and *n*. For item 2, say the picture names: *nine*, *nurse*, *pig*, *fork*, *necklace*, *nose*. Have children write *Nn* beside the pictures whose names begin with /n/. For item 3, have children draw something that starts with the /n/ sound.

Phonemic Awareness

Letter *Ff*

Have children listen and point as you name the pictures: *five*, *man*, *football*, *fan*, *hat*. Have them say the word *fish* and listen for the beginning sound /f/. Ask children to color each picture whose name begins the same as *fish*.

1. What can you see? 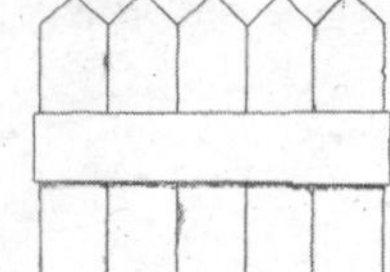

2. See what I can do. 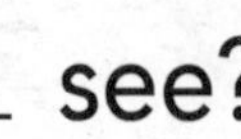 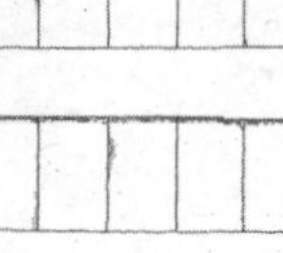

3. What can you see? 

4. Do you see what I see?  

Have children say the words *you* and *what* at the top of the page and trace them with a finger. Read the sentences aloud with children. Have them complete each sentence with the correct word. For sentence 4, have children draw a picture of something they see and then take turns sharing their pictures and rereading each sentence.

Comprehension

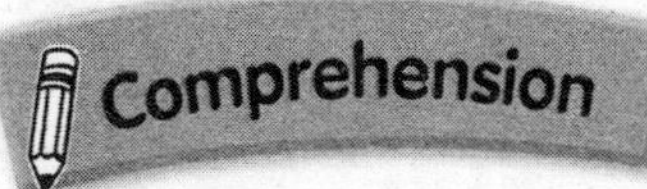

Author's Purpose

Reread the passage. Have children make a drawing to show something they learned from listening to the passage. Ask, *Is the author's purpose to tell a funny story or to help you learn something?* Encourage children to share their drawings and tell what they learned.

Phonemic Awareness

Letter *Ff*

Have children listen and point to the pictures as you name each one: *fan*, *fork*, *sun*, *fish*, *bike*, *five*. Have them say the word *foot* and listen for the beginning sound /f/. Have them color each picture whose name begins with the same beginning sound as in *foot*.

Phonics

Letter *Ff*

Have children point to the fish and say the beginning sound /f/. Have them practice writing capital *F* and small *f*. Name each picture: *fox*, *fire*, *lamp*, *table*, *football*. Then have children write *Ff* beside the pictures whose names begin with /f/.

Phonemic Awareness

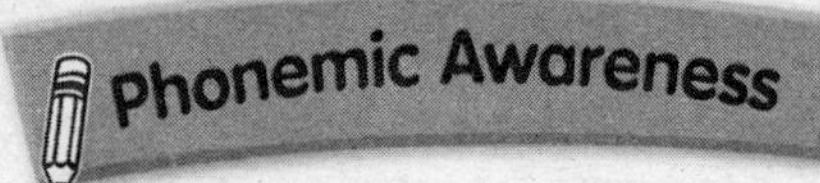

Letter *Bb*

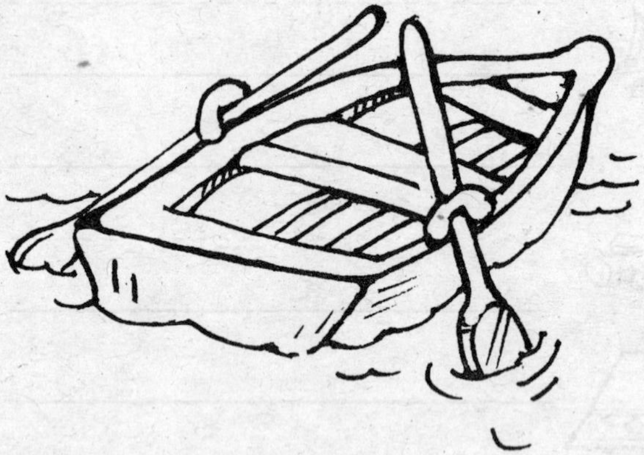

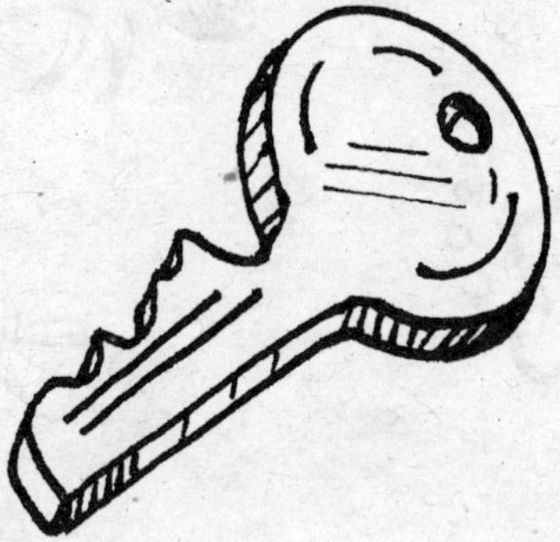

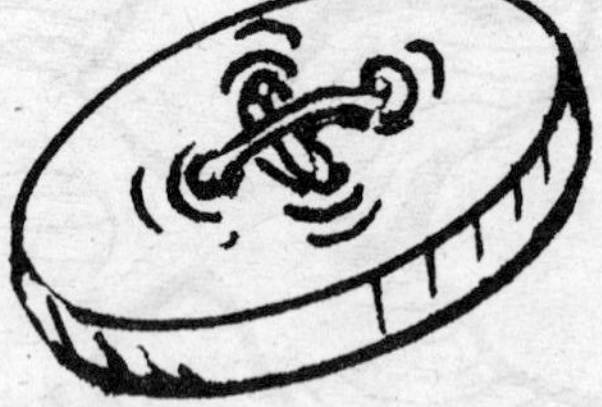

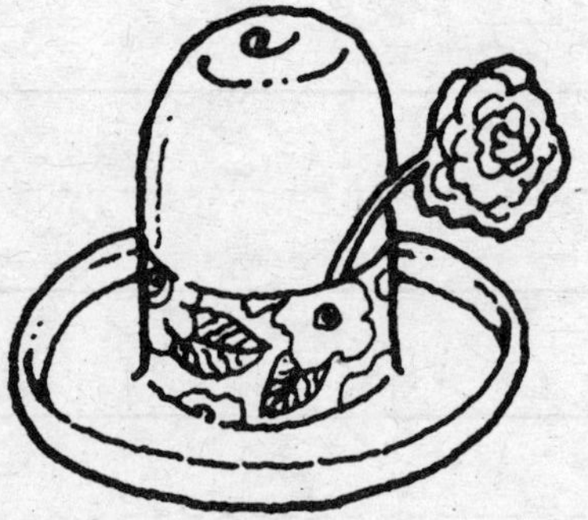

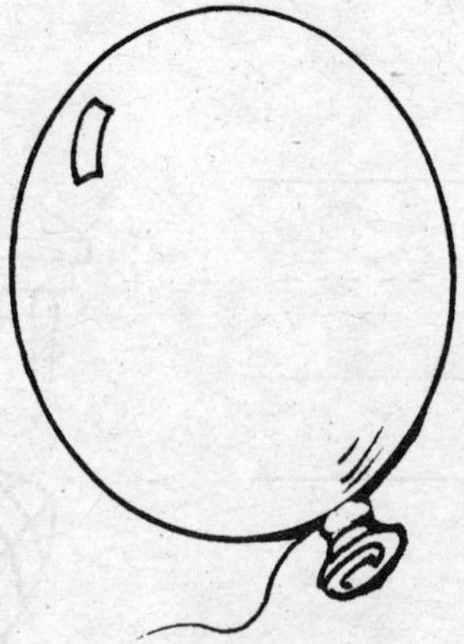

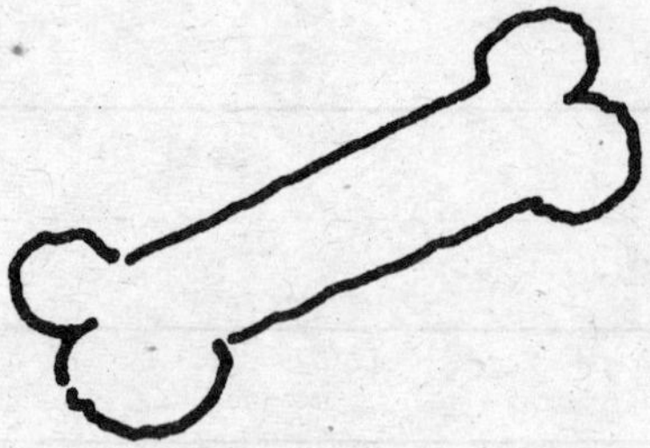

Have children listen and point to each picture as you name it: *boat*, *key*, *button*, *hat*, *balloon*, *bone*. Have them circle each picture whose name begins with the /b/ sound and place an X over any picture that does not begin with the /b/ sound.

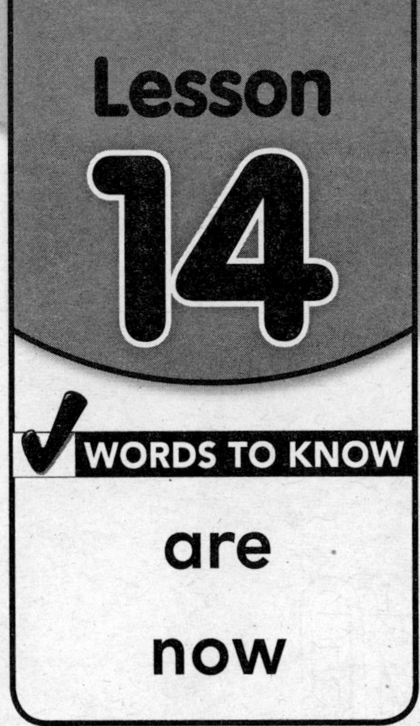

1. We are ____.

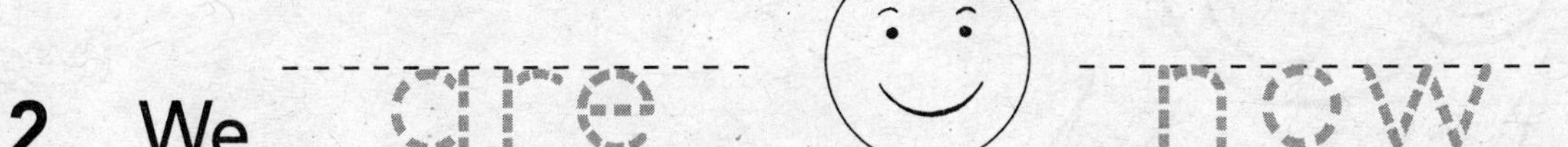

2. We are ____ now.

3. The ____ are dry.

4. The ____ are wet now.

Do sentence 1 with children. Have them trace the word *are*. Read the sentence aloud together. Repeat the procedure for sentences 2–4.

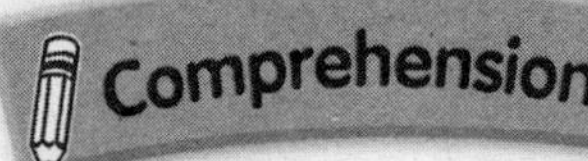

Cause and Effect

Remind children that rain can cause things to happen. Have them circle images that show what rain can cause. Do the first two with children. Then discuss why children did or did not circle each image.

Phonemic Awareness

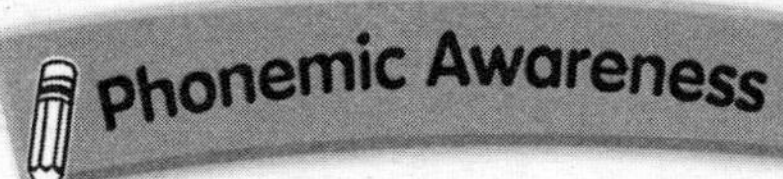

Letter *Bb*

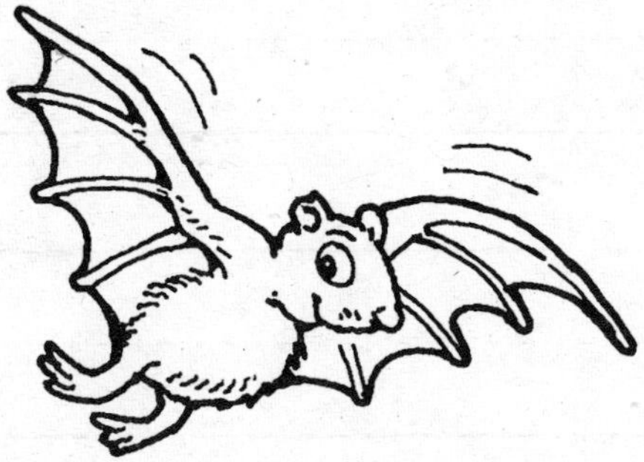
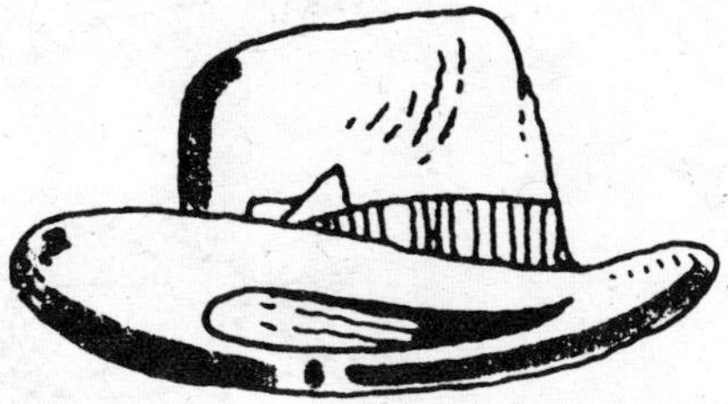
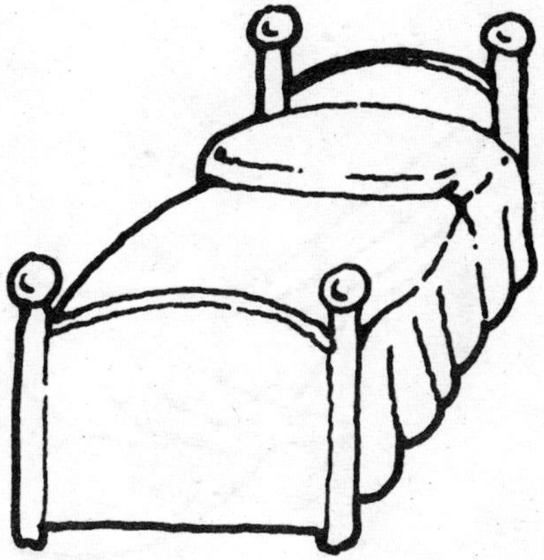
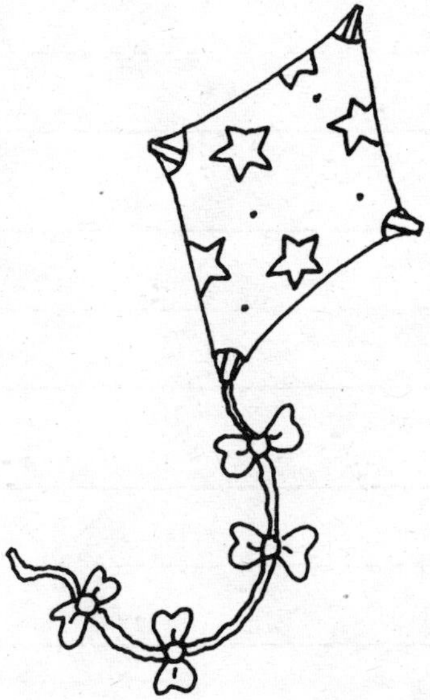
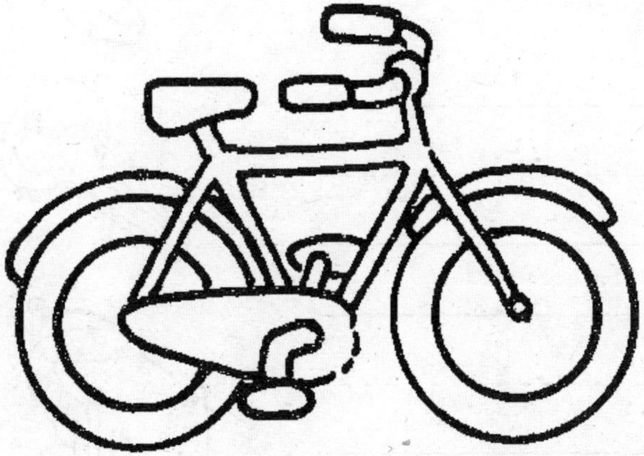
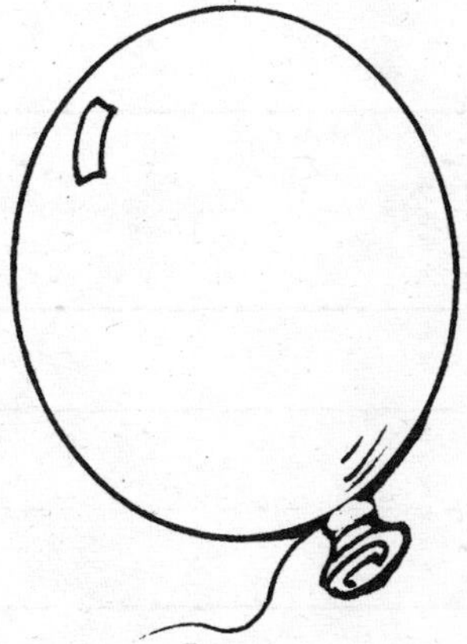

Have children listen and point as you name the pictures: *bat*, *hat*, *bed*, *kite*, *bike*, *balloon*. Have them say the word *baseball* and listen for the beginning sound /b/. Have them color each picture whose name begins the same as *baseball*.

phonics Letter *Bb*

Have children point to the bird and say the beginning sound /b/. Have them practice writing capital *B* and small *b*. Then name each picture: *boat*, *fish*, *banana*, *key*, *bed*. Have children write *Bb* beside the pictures whose names begin with /b/.

Blend Phonemes

Say the sounds in the name of each picture on the page: *cow, duck, sun, fish, pig, cat*. Each time, have children blend the sounds, say the word, and point to the picture named. Children can then color the pictures as they practice saying and blending the sounds in each word.

Lesson
15

WORDS TO KNOW

are
come
me
my
now
what
with
you

1. I am ______ my [picture of dad].

with you

2. We ______ at the [picture of zoo].

me are

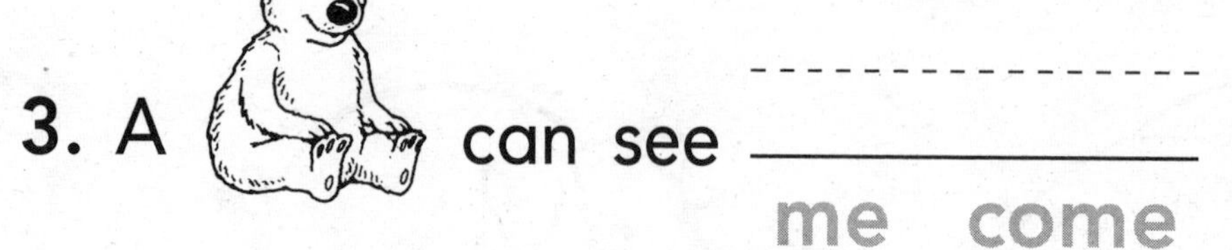

3. A [picture of bear] can see ______.

me come

4. We see a [picture of lion] ______.

now what

Read sentence 1 with each of the word choices: I am [with, you] my dad. Have children point to and write the correct word. Then read the sentence aloud together. Continue with sentences 2–4.

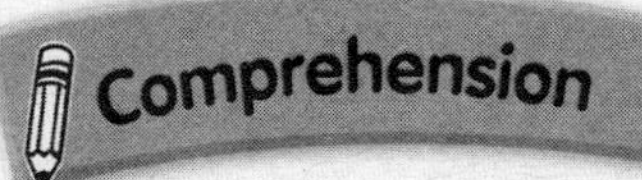

Sequence of Events

Remind children that stories have a beginning, a middle, and an end. Talk about each picture. Tell children to put the numbers 1, 2, and 3 in each box to show what happened at the beginning, in the middle, and at the end of the story.

Phonemic Awareness

Blend Phonemes

Tell children you will say the sounds in the name of something in the picture: /h/ /ă/ /t/.
Have children blend the sounds, say the word, and circle the hat in the picture.
Repeat with *cat*, *man*, *bat*, *ant*, *map*. Have children color the picture when they are done.

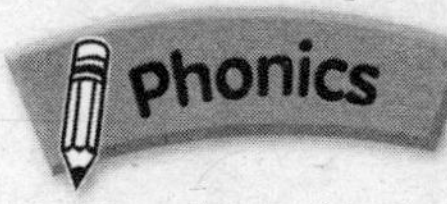

Blend Words

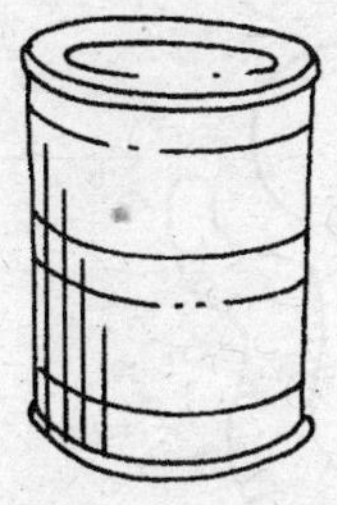

cat

can

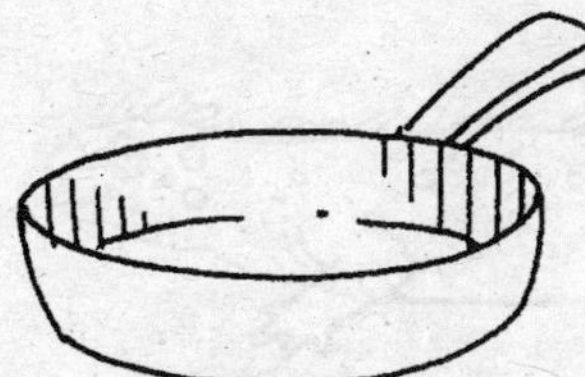

pat

pan

nap

pan

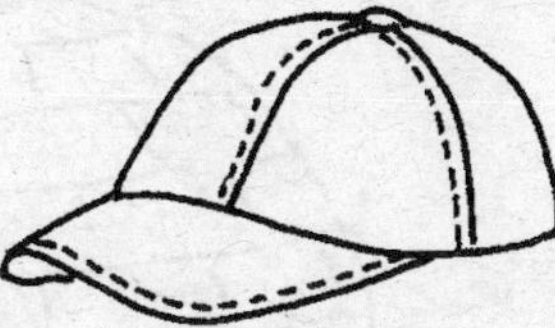

cap

map

Name the pictures: *can*, *pan*, *nap*, *cap*. Have children read the words beside each picture, circle the word that names the picture, and write it on the line. Do the first one together.

Phonemic Awareness

Letter *Ii*

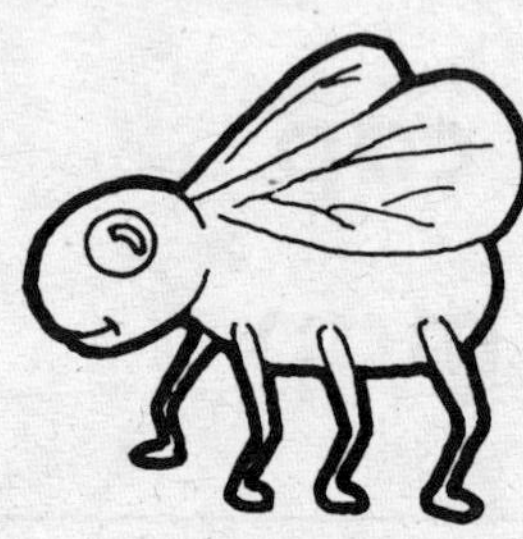

Have children listen and point to each picture as you name it: *iguana*, *brush*, *inchworm*, *insect*, *igloo*, *book*. Have them circle each picture whose name begins with the /ĭ/ sound and place an X over any picture that does not begin with the /ĭ/ sound.

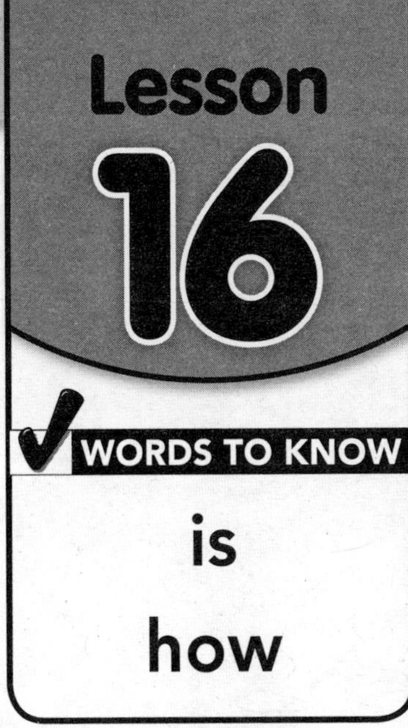

1. The cat is .

2. The cat is .

3. I know how to .

4. I know how to .

Have children read the words *is* and *how*. Complete sentence 1 together. Have children trace the word *is* and read the sentence aloud. Children can complete sentence 2 on their own. For sentences 3 and 4, read the sentences and work with children to fill in the missing word *how*. Then have children read the sentences aloud.

Comprehension

Details

Have children circle the pictures that show details of the story about Eva moving into a new house.
Have them draw lines to connect the story details to the main idea in the middle circle.

Letter *Ii*

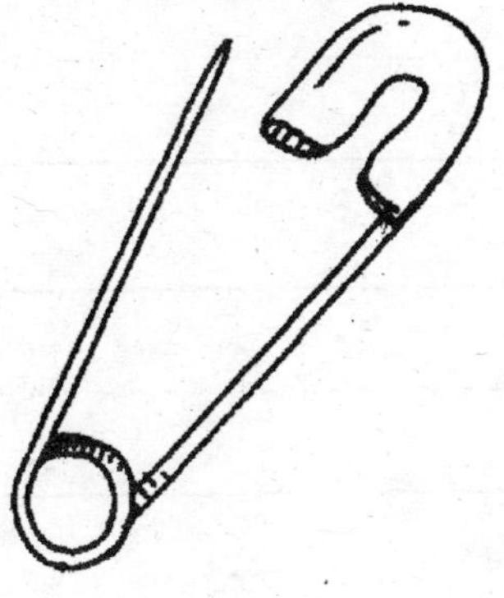

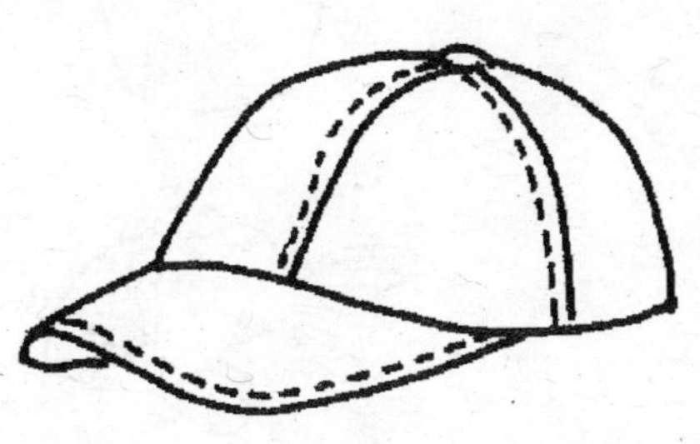

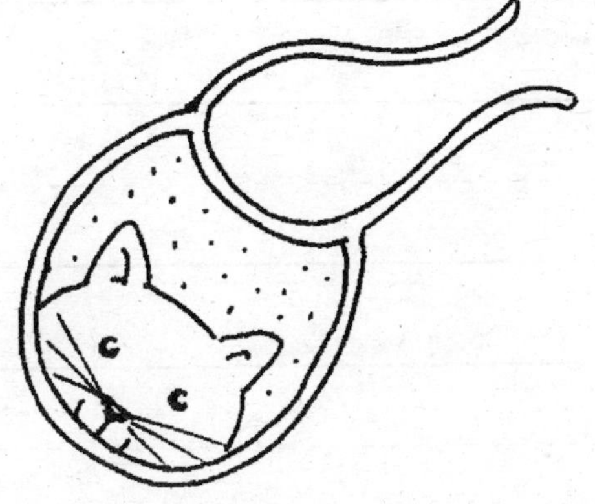

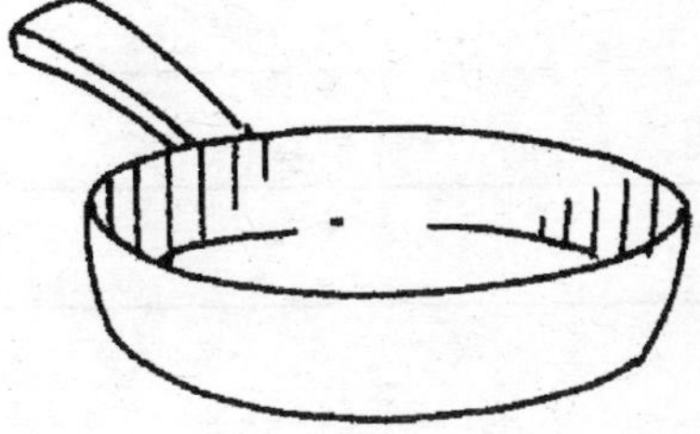

Have children point as you name the pictures: *pin*, *cap*, *igloo*, *bib*, *pig*, and *pan*. Have them say the word *pin* and listen for the picture names that have the /i/ sound. Then have children color each picture whose name has the same sound as *igloo*.

Phonics Letter *Ii*

Have children point to the pin and say the middle sound /ĭ/. Have them practice writing capital *I* and small *i*. Then name the objects: *cup*, *fish*, *mat*, *pig*, and *bin*. Have children write *Ii* beside the pictures whose names have the /ĭ/ sound.

Phonemic Awareness

Letter *Gg*

Have children point to the pictures as you name them: *game*, *gate*, *gas*, *pan*, *guitar*, *cap*, and *goat*. Have them say the word *game* and listen for the beginning sound /g/. Then have children color each picture whose name begins with the same sound as *game*.

Lesson 17

✓ WORDS TO KNOW

find

this

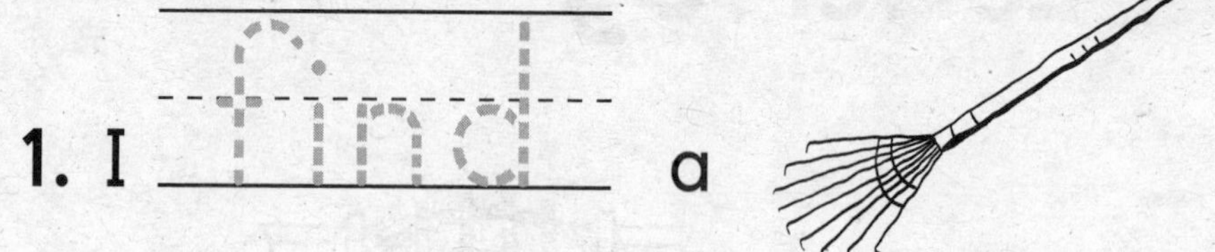

1. I find a [picture].

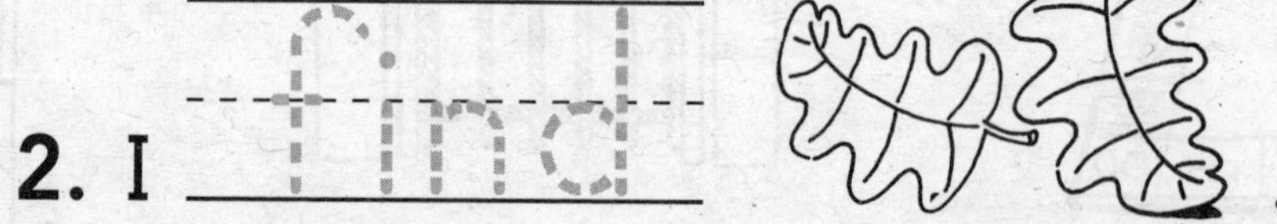

2. I find [picture].

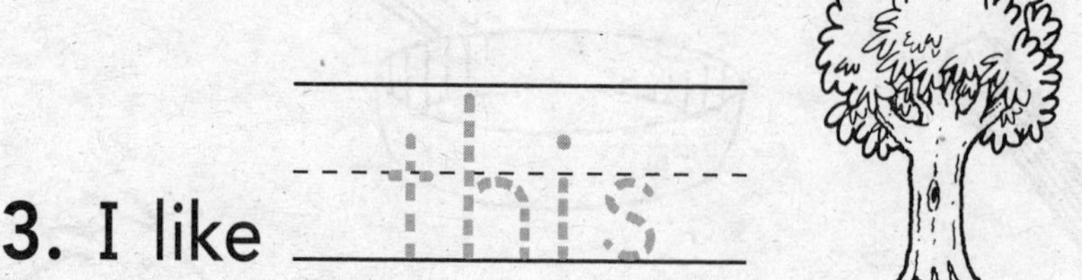

3. I like this [picture].

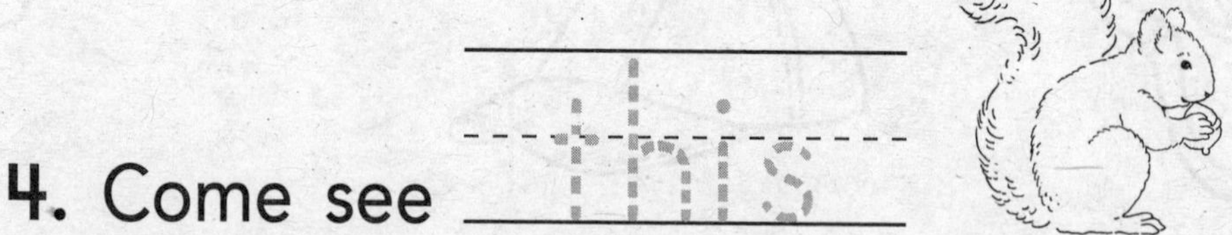

4. Come see this [picture].

Have children point to and read the words *find* and *this*. Do sentence 1 with children. Have them trace the word *find* and then read the sentence aloud. Repeat for sentences 2–4.

Comprehension

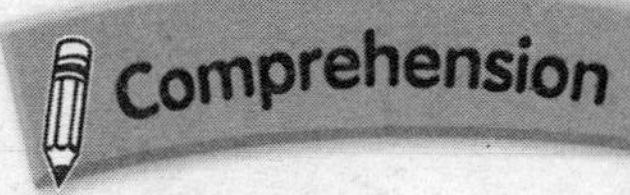

Draw Conclusions

1.

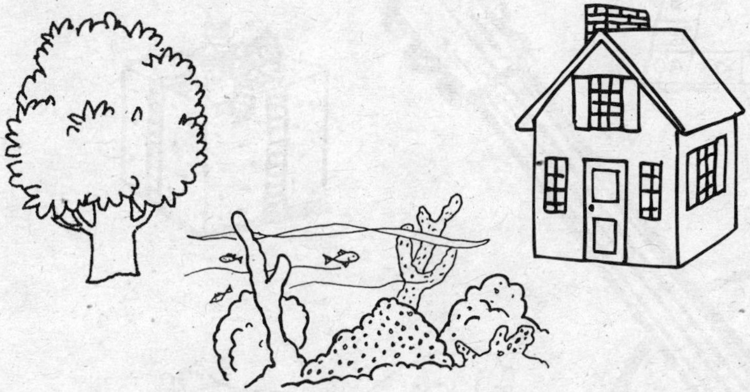

2.

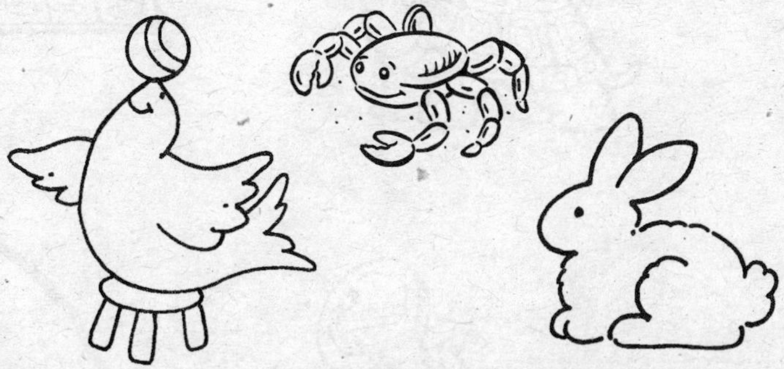

3.

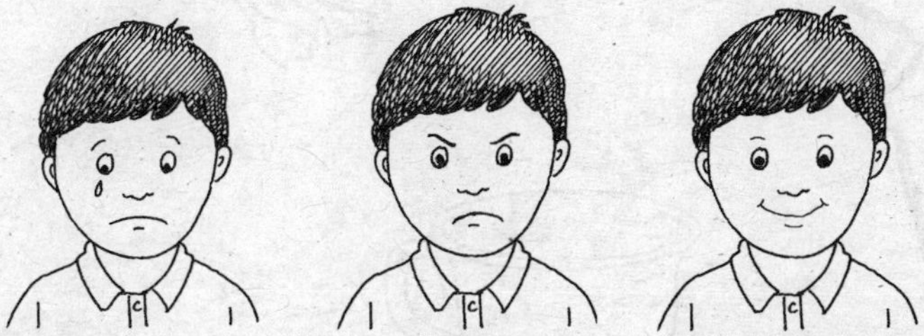

4.

Tell children to use clues from the story to answer questions about Willy the Crab and his best friend Tif. For item 1, ask children to circle the picture that shows where Willy and Tif live. For item 2, have children circle the picture that shows the type of animal that Tif is. For item 3, have children circle the picture that shows how Willy feels about Tif. For item 4, invite children to draw a picture of Willy and Tif playing a game.

Phonemic Awareness

Letter *Gg*

Have children point to the pictures as you name them: *turtle*, *game*, *gift*, *key*, *guitar*, *goose*, *goat*, and *cup*. Have them say the word *guitar* and listen for the beginning sound /g/. Then have children color each picture whose name has the same beginning sound as *guitar*.

Phonics

Letter *Gg*

Have children point to the guitar and say the beginning sound /g/. Have them practice writing capital *G* and small *g*. Then name the objects: *hose*, *gas*, *gum*, *bee*, and *gate*. Have children write *Gg* beside the pictures whose names begin wit the /g/ sound.

Phonemic Awareness

Letter *Rr*

Have children point to the pictures as you name them: *clock*, *ring*, *can*, *rabbit*, *mouse*, *rake*, and *rug*. Then have children circle the objects that begin with the /r/ sound. Have children draw something else that begins with the /r/ sound.

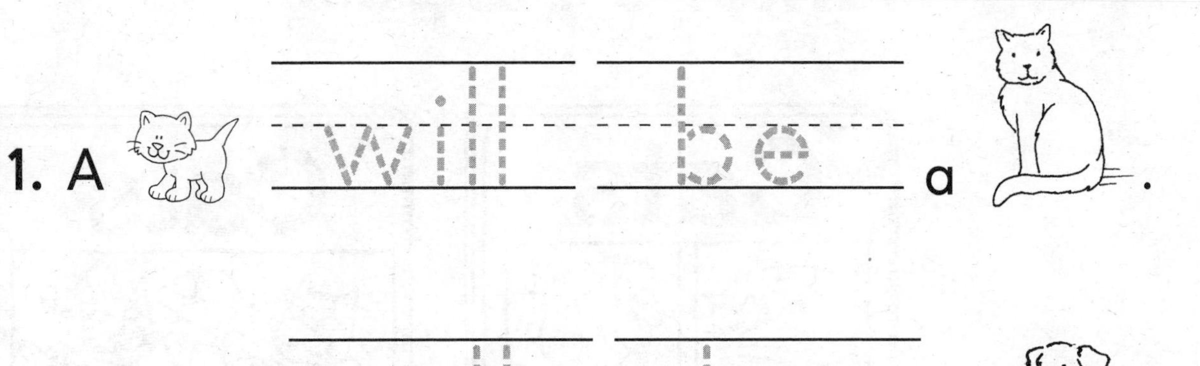

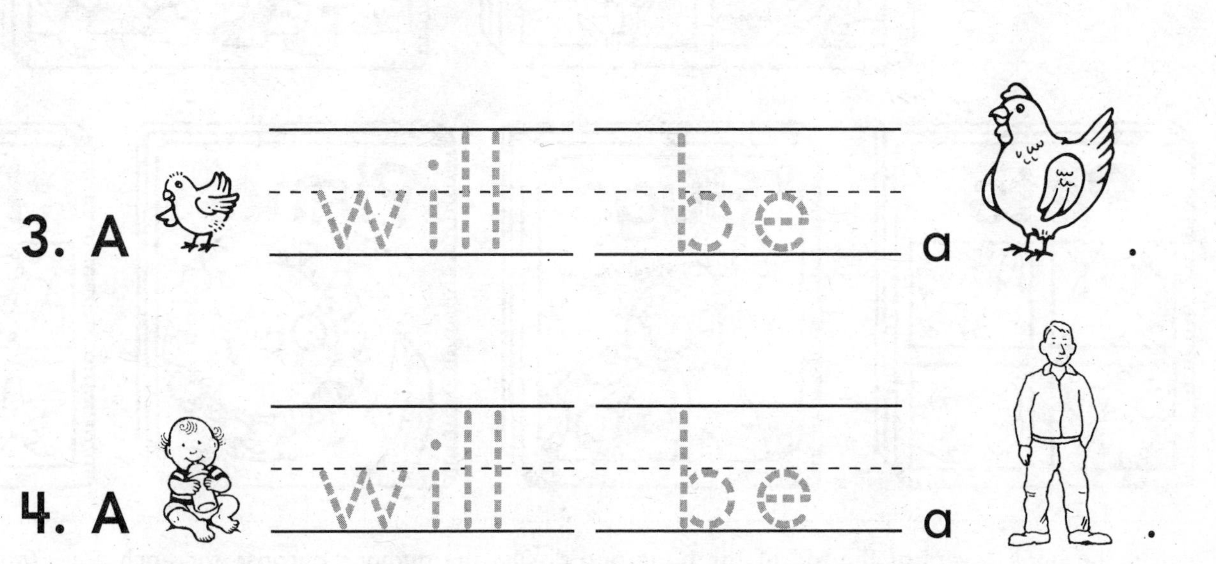

Have children say the words *will* and *be*. Do sentence 1 together. Have them trace the words *will* and *be* and then read the sentence aloud. Discuss how a kitten will be a cat when it gets older. Ask, *What will you be when you grow up?* Then have children complete sentences 2–4 on their own and read them.

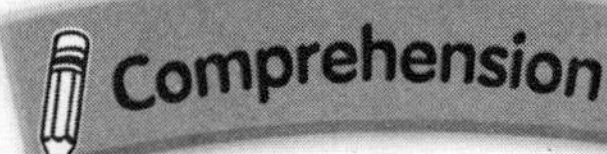

Author's Purpose

Point to the book covers at the top of the page and discuss the author's purpose for each. Say, *This cover shows different types of real cats. This author wants me to learn something about cats.* Point to the other cover and say, *This cover shows cats wearing clothes. This author wrote this book to tell a funny story.* Discuss the other book covers. Have children use picture clues to figure out the author's purpose. Have them draw a line connecting each at the top of the page with books at the bottom that have a similar purpose.

Phonemic Awareness

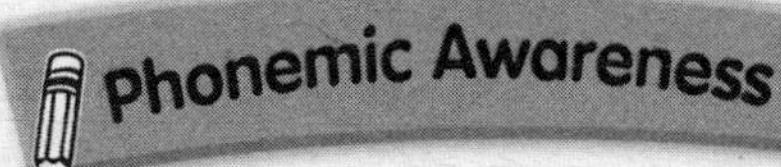

Letter *Rr*

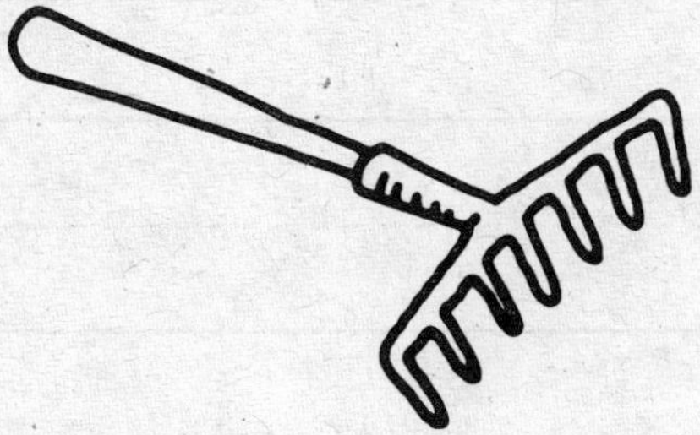

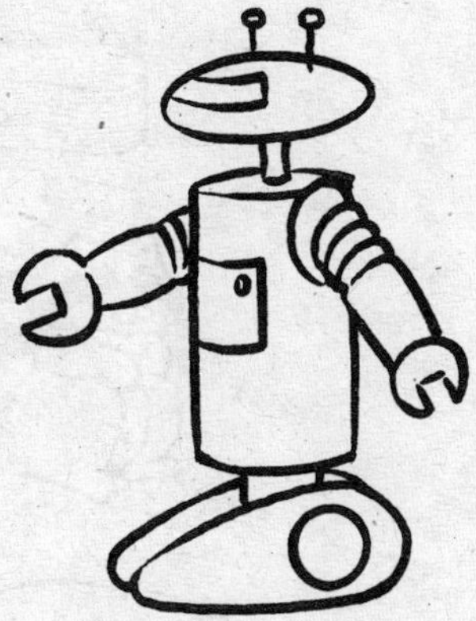

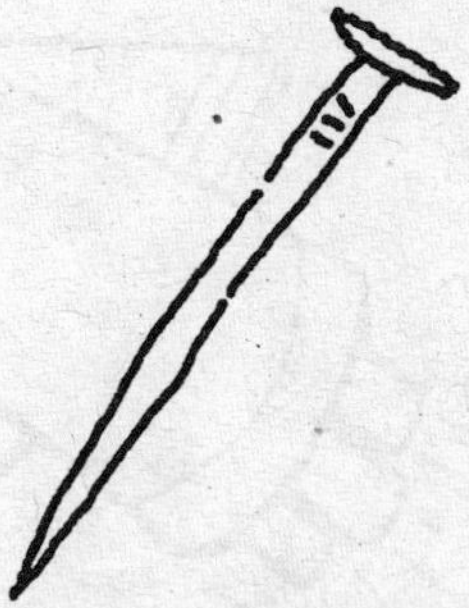

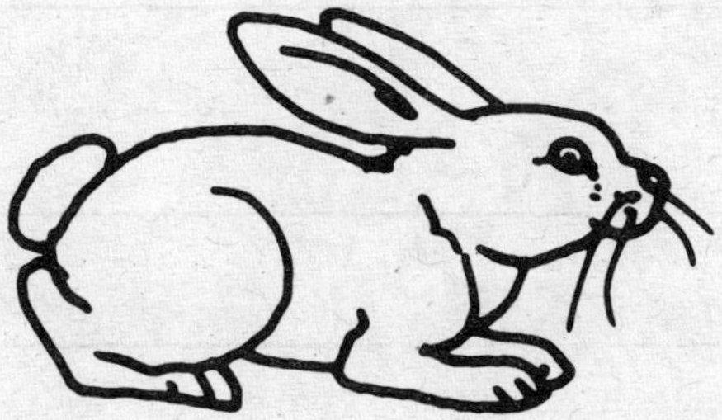

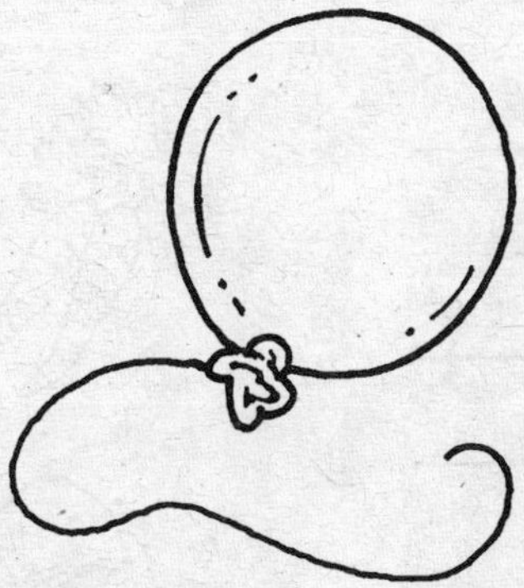

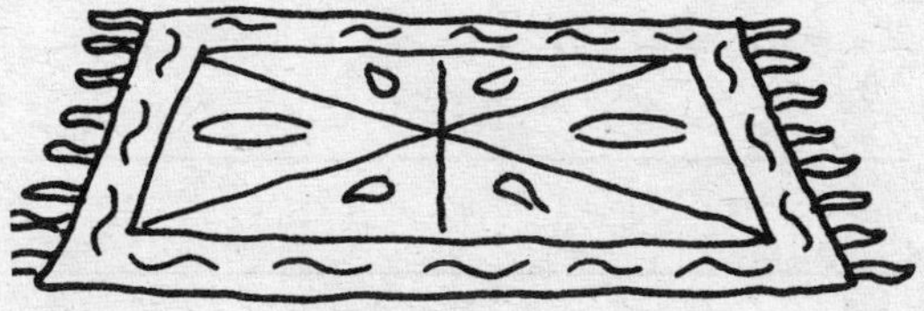

Have children listen and point to the pictures as you name each one: ***rake***, ***robot***, ***nail***, ***rabbit***, ***balloon***, ***rug***. Have them say the word *rake* and listen for the beginning sound /r/. Then have them color each picture whose name begins the same as *rake*.

Phonics

Letter *Rr*

Have children point to the rocket and say the name and the beginning sound /r/. Have them practice writing capital *R* and small *r*. Name each picture: *ribbon*, *raccoon*, *van*, *carrot*, *rock*. Then have children write *Rr* beside the pictures whose names begin with the /r/ sound.

Letter *Dd*

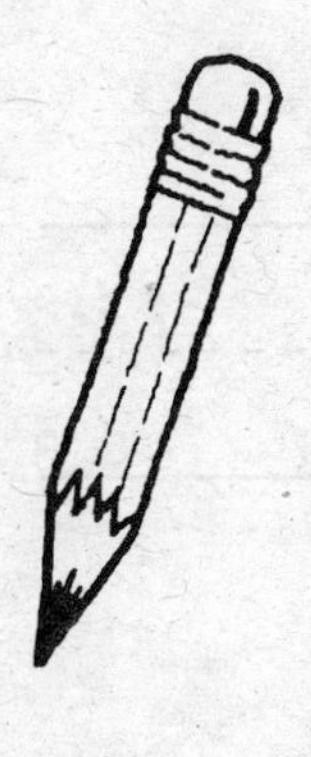

Have children listen and point to each picture as you name it: *dinosaur*, *pencil*, *dishes*, *desk*, *deer*, *book*. Have them circle each picture whose name begins with the /d/ sound and place an X over any picture that does not begin with the /d/ sound.

Lesson 19

✓ WORDS TO KNOW

go

for

1. I ______________ to  .

2. I ______________ to a  .

3. A 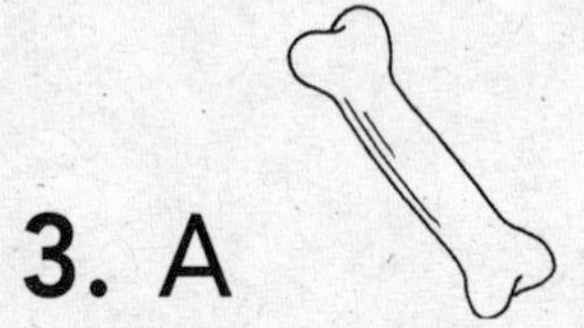 is ______________ a  .

4. A  is ______________ a  .

Have children point to and say the words *go* and *for*. Read sentence 1 with each of the words: *I [go, for] to school*. Have children write the correct word to complete the sentence. Have them read the completed sentence aloud. Continue with sentences 2–4.

Comprehension

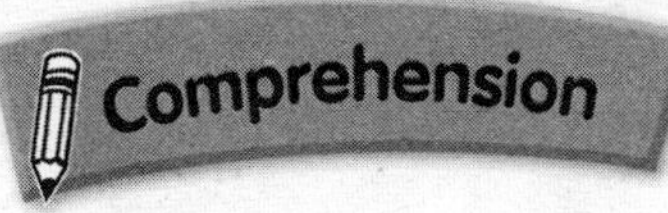

Cause and Effect

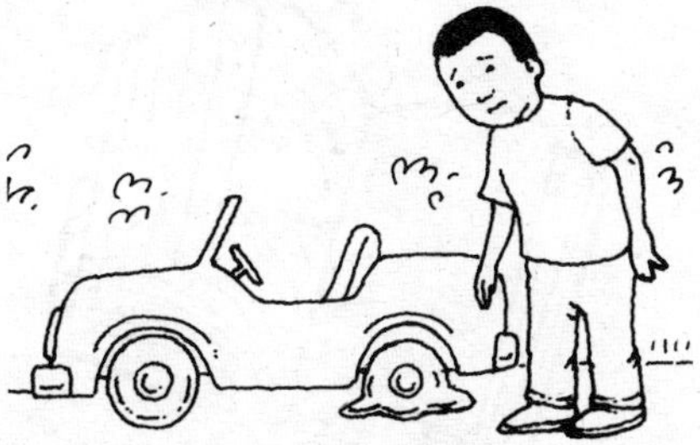

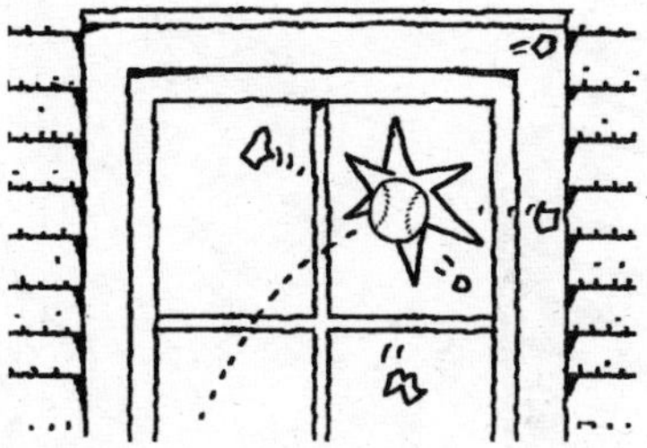

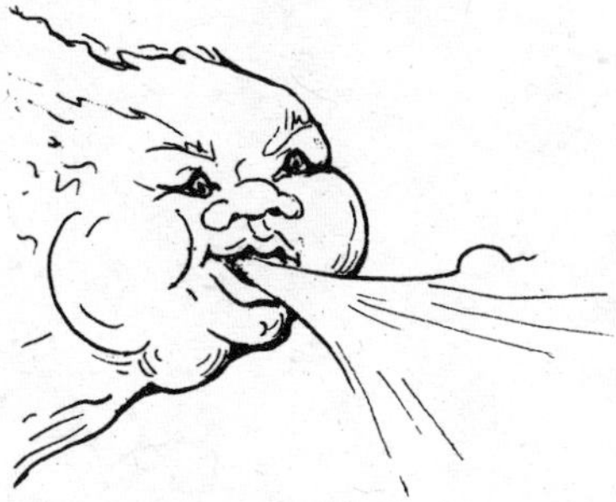

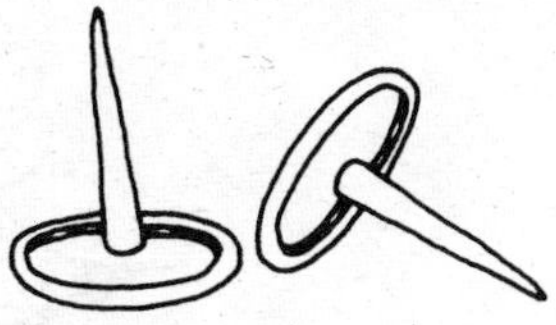

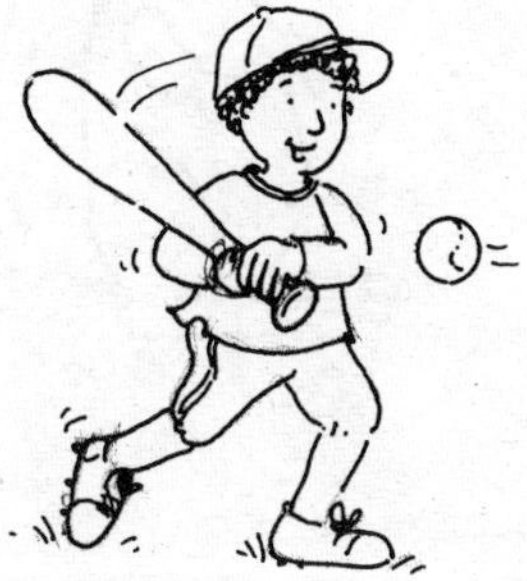

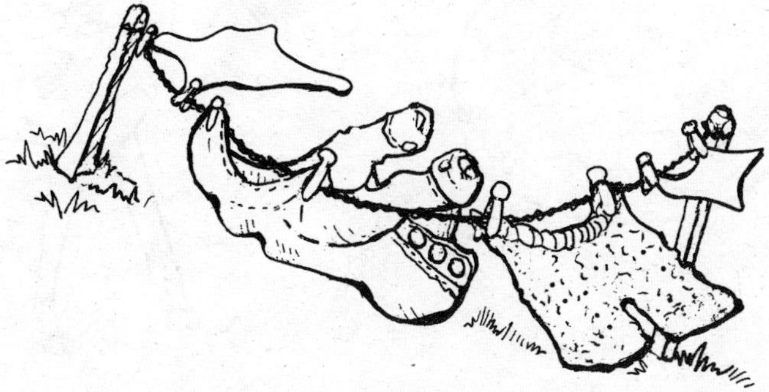

Talk with children about each picture. Then have children draw lines to connect what happened with what caused it to happen.

Letter *Dd*

Have children listen and point as you name the pictures: *dishes*, *doll*, *book*, *donut*, *deer*, *mouse*.
Have them color each picture whose name begins with the sound /d/.

Letter *Dd*

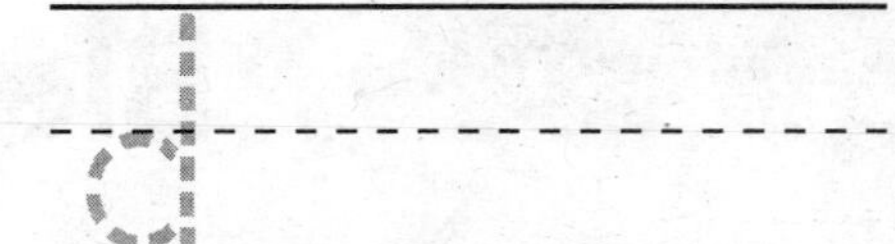

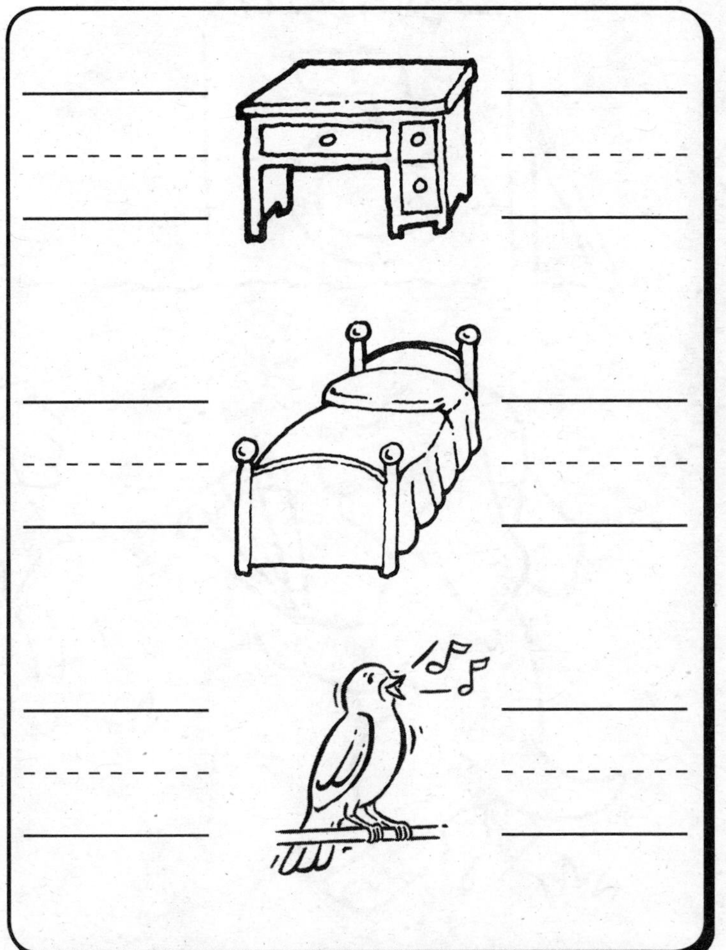

Have children practice writing *D* and *d* at the top of the page. Then have children say each picture name: *dog, dishes, deer, desk, bed, bird.* Say, *If you hear /d/ at the beginning of the picture name, write* d *on the lines in front of the picture. If the name ends with /d/, write* d *on the lines after the picture.*

Phonemic Awareness

Blend Phonemes

Say the sounds in one of the picture names: /f/ /ă/ /n/. Have children blend the sounds, say the word, and color the object red. Repeat for *five*, *fish*, *gate*, and *dog*.

Lesson 20

WORDS TO KNOW

is
how
find
this
will
be
go
for

1. The ______ hot.
   how is

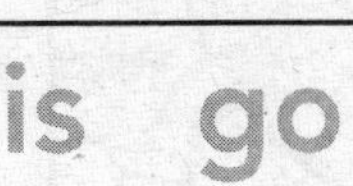

2. I ______ to the ______ .
   is go

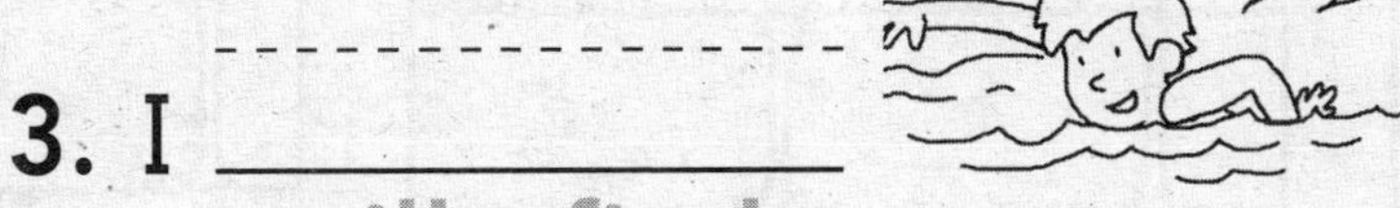

3. I ______ ______ .
   will find

4. This is ______ I ______ .
   for how

Read sentence 1 with each of the word choices: *The sun [how, is] hot*. Continue the process for the remaining sentences and pictures (beach, swim, dig). Then have children read the story aloud.

Comprehension

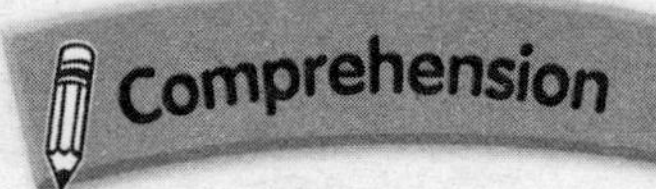

Sequence of Events

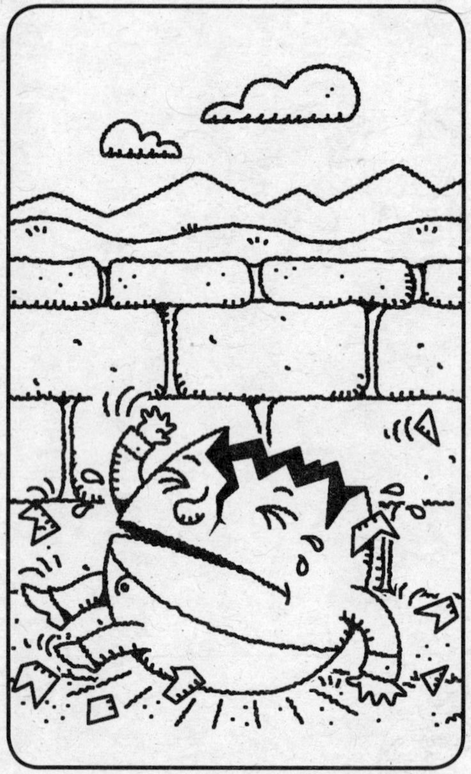

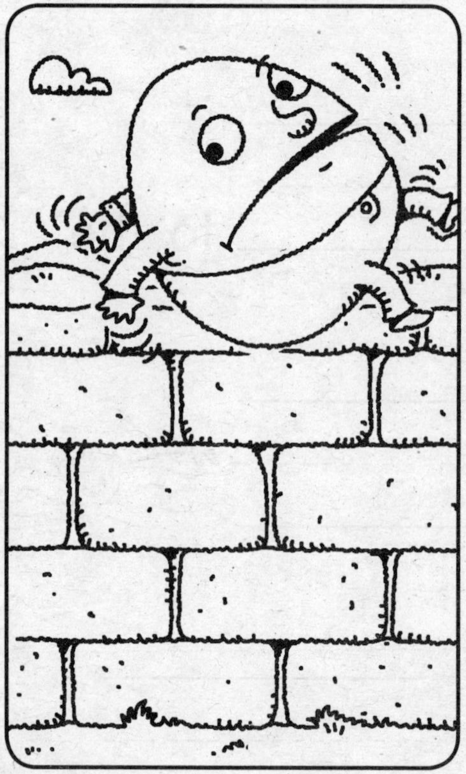

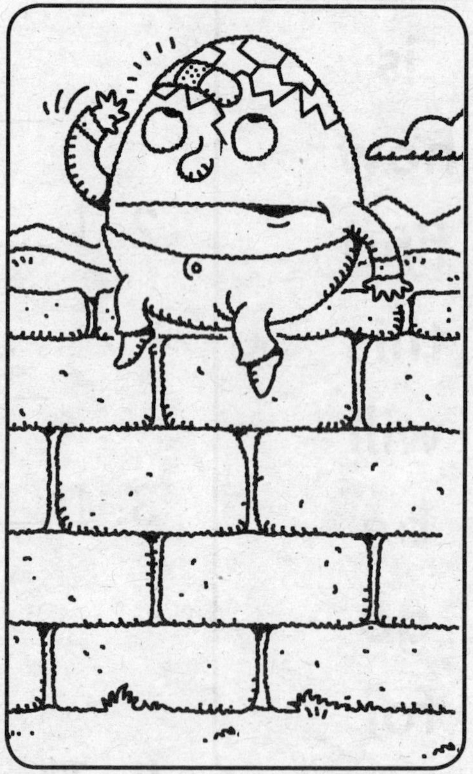

Remind children that stories have a beginning, middle, and end. Talk about each picture. Tell children to put the numbers *1*, *2*, and *3* in each box to show what happened at the beginning, in the middle, and at the end of the rhyme.

Phonemic Awareness

Blend Phonemes

Tell children you will say the sounds in the name of something they see in the picture: /m/ /ă/ /t/. Have children blend the sounds, say the word, and circle the picture. Repeat with *bag*, *dad*, *map*, *pig*, and *pin*.

Phonics

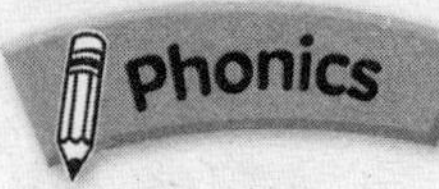

Blend Words

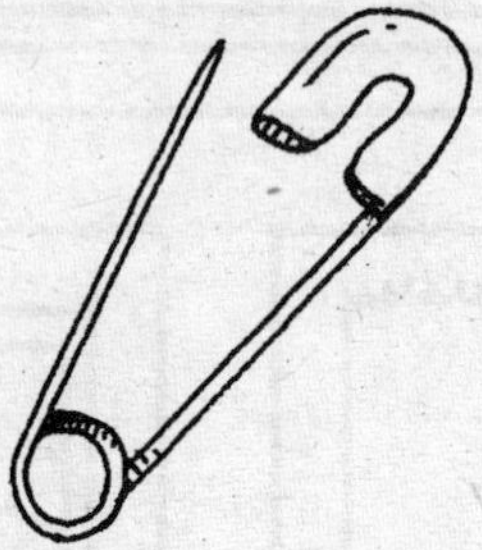

pin

dig

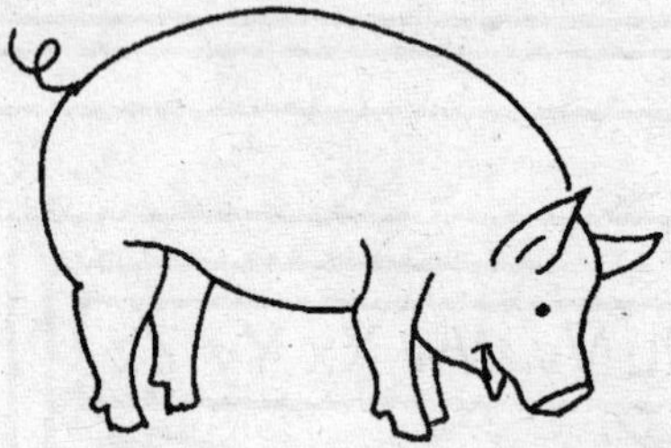

lip

pig

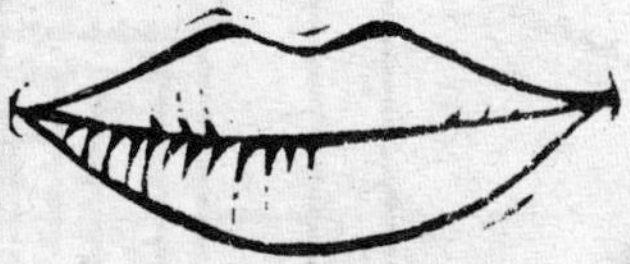

sit

lip

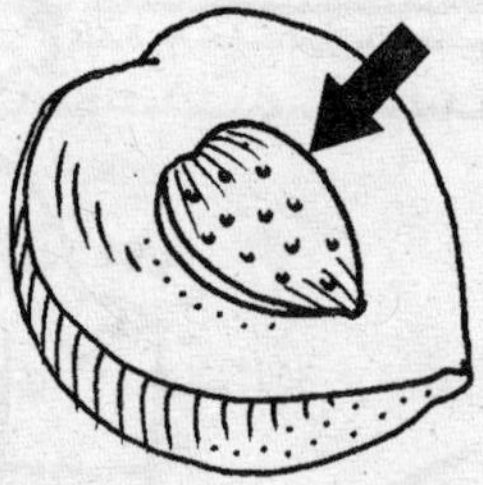

pit

pan

Name the pictures: *pin*, *pig*, *lip*, *pit*. Have children segment and blend sounds to read the words beside each picture. Have them circle the word that matches the picture, and write it on the line. Do the first one together.

Letter *Oo*

Have children listen and point to each picture as you name it: *octopus, kite, ox, ostrich, otter, van.* Have them circle each picture whose name begins with the /ŏ/ sound and place an X over any picture that does not begin with the /ŏ/ sound.

Lesson 21

WORDS TO KNOW

make

play

1. We can make a  .

2. We like to play  .

3. We can make a 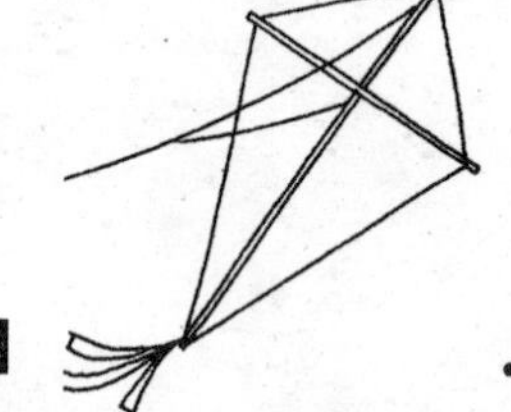 .

4. We like to 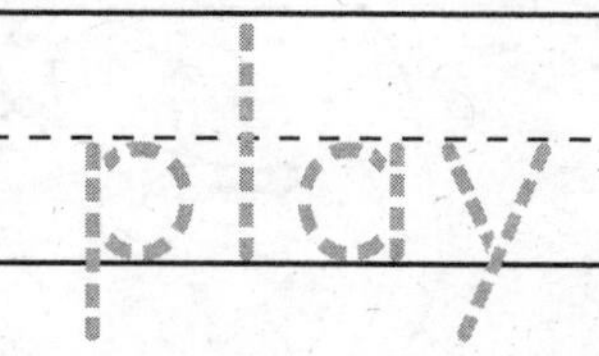  .

Have children say the word *make*. Complete sentence 1 with children. Have them trace the word *make* and read the sentence aloud. For sentence 2, have children say the word *play*. Then have them trace the word *play* and read the sentence aloud. Children do 3 and 4 on their own.

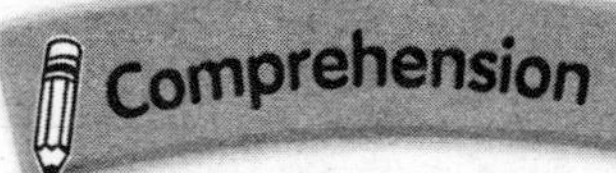

Understanding Characters

For item 1, have children circle the picture that shows what Flip likes to play with. For item 2, have them circle the picture that shows how they think Flip feels when the cats do not play with him. For item 3, have children circle the picture that shows what Flip's family brings home. Then read sentence 4 with children and ask, *What do you think Flip and the new dog will play together?* Have them draw a picture to share their ideas.

Letter *Oo*

Have children point as you name the pictures: *otter*, *fox*, *hen*, *bike*, *fan*, *box*. Have them say the word *fox* and listen for the /ŏ/ sound. Have children color each picture whose name contains the /ŏ/ sound.

Phonics

Letter *Oo*

Have children point to the pot and say the sound /ŏ/. Have them practice writing capital *O* and small *o*. Say the remaining picture names aloud: *fox*, *hen*, *mop*, *doll*. Then have children write *Oo* beside the pictures whose names contain the /ŏ/ sound.

Letters *Xx*, *Jj*

For question 1, have children point as you name the pictures: *fox*, *apple*, *box*, *cat*. Have them say the word *fox* and listen for the /ks/ sound. Have them color each picture whose name contains the /ks/ sound. For question 2, have children point as you name the pictures: *jug*, *sun*, *goat*, *jar*. Have them say the word *jug* and listen for the /j/ sound. Have them color each picture whose name begins with the /j/ sound.

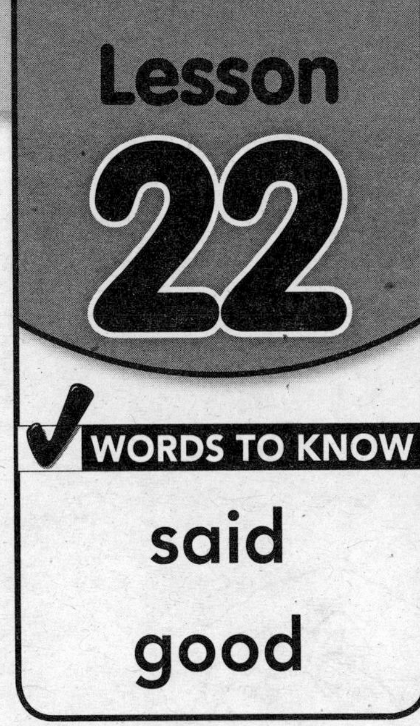

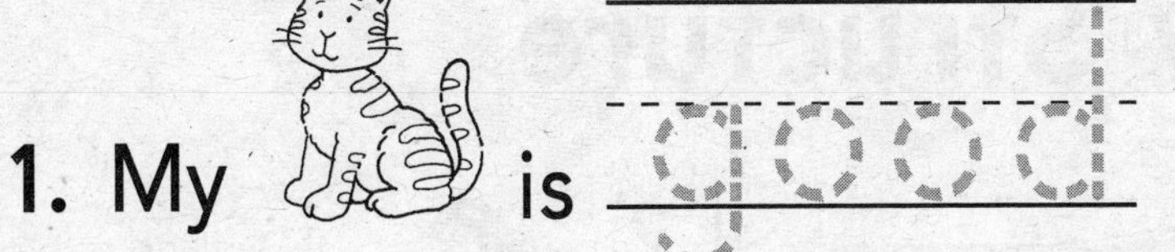

1. My [cat] is good .

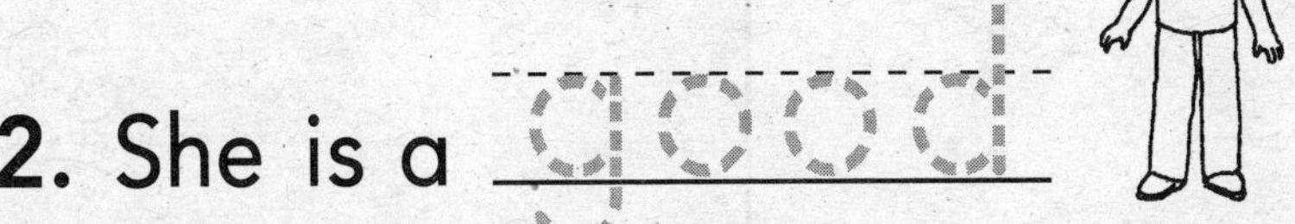

2. She is a good [girl] .

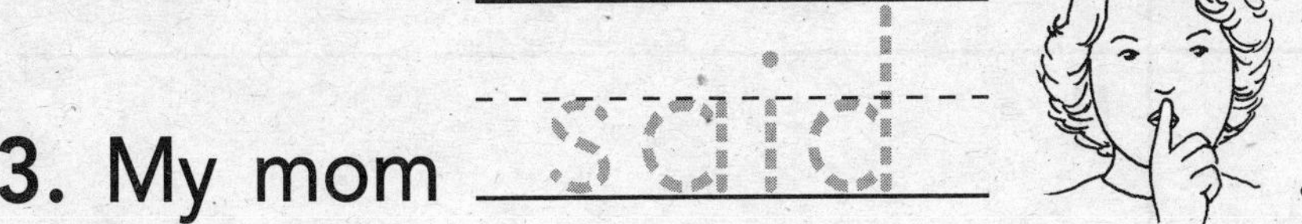

3. My mom said [ssshhh] .

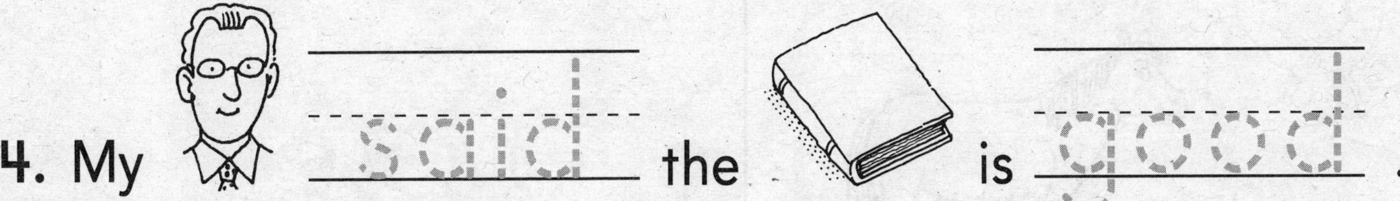

4. My [dad] said the [book] is good .

Point to the Words to Know. Have children say the words with you. Guide children to name the pictures on the page: *cat*, *girl*, *ssshhh*, *dad*. Do sentence 1 with children. Have them trace the word *good* and read the sentence aloud. Children complete 2–4 on their own.

Comprehension

Story Structure

1.

2.

3.

4.

Have children circle the picture in question 1 that shows what the character looks like. Have children circle the picture in question 2 that shows where the story takes place. Tell children to circle the picture in question 3 that shows the character's problem. For question 4, have children draw a picture of what they think will happen at the end of the story.

Letters *Xx*, *Jj*

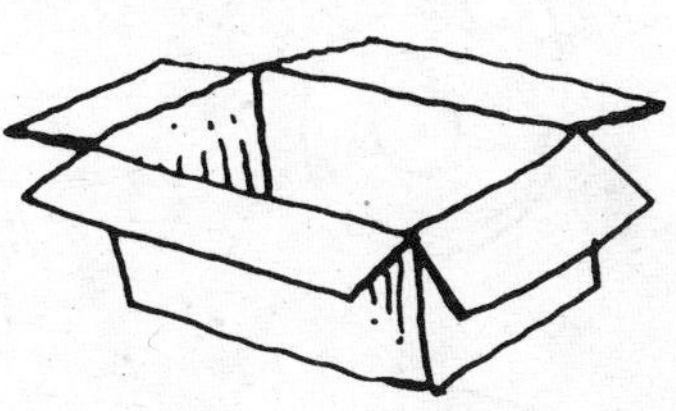

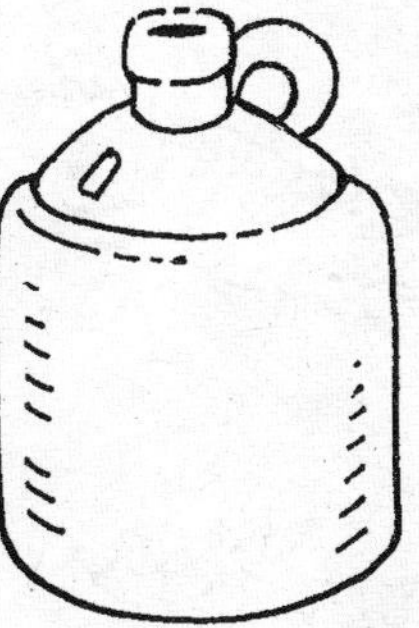

Have children point as you name the pictures in the first row: *six*, *fox*, *mug*, *box*. Tell children to color the pictures whose names end with the /ks/ sound. Have children point as you name the pictures in the second row: *jet*, *jam*, *tree*, *jug*. Tell children to color the pictures whose names begin with the /j/ sound.

Phonics Letters *Xx*, *Jj*

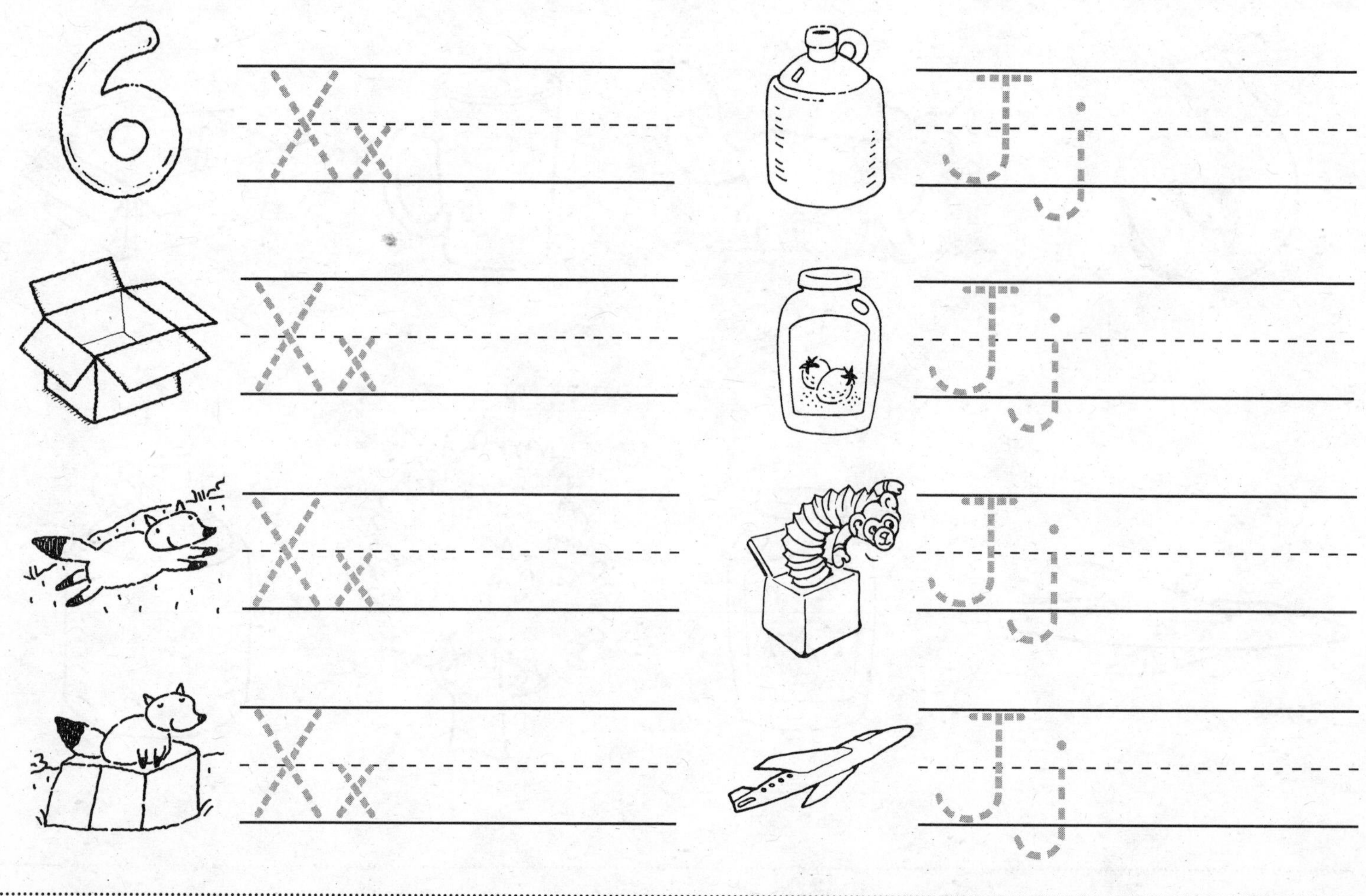

Have children point to the six and say the end sound /ks/. Have them practice writing capital *X* and small *x*. Then have children write *Xx* beside the pictures whose names end with /ks/. Repeat the process for the letter *Jj*.

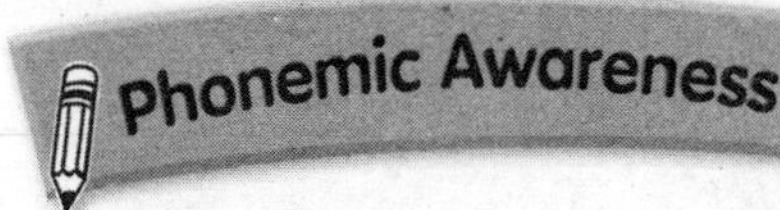

Letter *Ee*

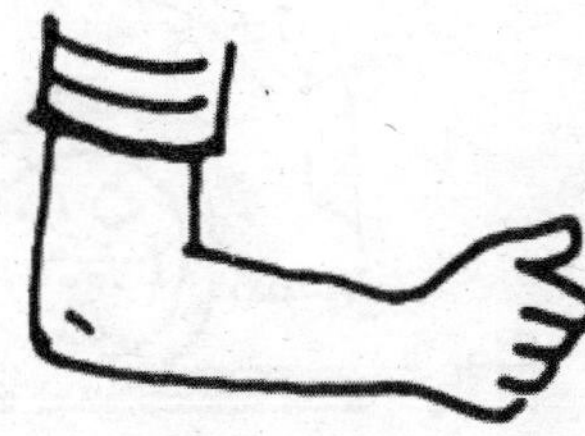

Have children point as you name the pictures: *eggs, hat, elephant, pig, elbow, boy*. Have them color the pictures whose names begin with the /ĕ/ sound. Have children say the names of the objects that begin with the /ĕ/ sound.

Lesson

23

✓ WORDS TO KNOW

she

all

1. We ___all___ get in the van.

2. Can ___she___ get in?

3. Will ___she___ fit?

4. We can ___all___ fit.

Have children read the words *she* and *all*. Complete sentence 1 with children. Have them trace the word *all* and read the sentence aloud. Repeat procedure for sentences 2–4.

Comprehension

Sequence of Events

Discuss the story with children. Have children use the first box to draw a picture of what Mina does in the beginning of the story. Have them use the center box to draw what happens in the middle of the story and the third box to draw the story's ending. Have children use their drawings to retell the sequence of events in the story.

Letter *Ee*

Have children point to the pictures as you name them: *web*, *net*, *egg*, *pig*, *pan*, and *bed*. Have them say the word *egg* and listen for the beginning sound /ĕ/. Then have children color each picture whose name has the same sound as *egg*.

Phonics

Letter *Ee*

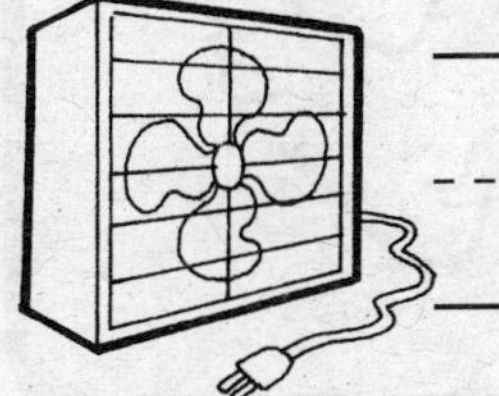

Have children point to the elephant and say the name and the beginning sound /ĕ/. Have them practice writing capital *E* and small *e*. Name each remaining picture: *leg*, *hen*, *log*, *pen*, *fan*. Tell children to write *Ee* beside the pictures whose names have the /ĕ/ sound in the middle.

Phonemic Awareness

Letters *Hh*, *Kk*

1.

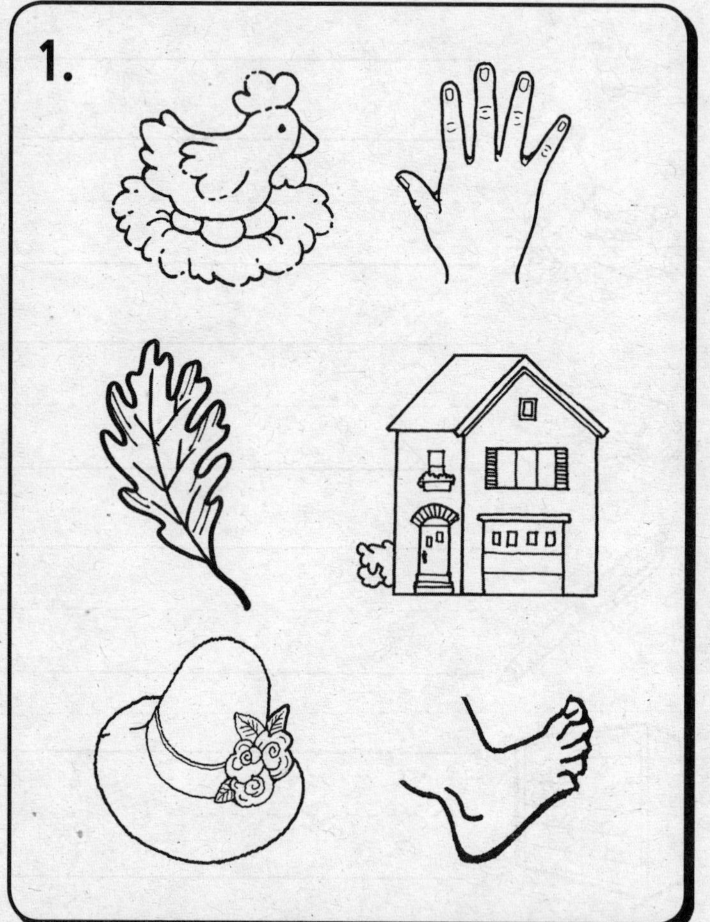

2.

Have children listen and point as you name the pictures in the first box: *hen*, *hand*, *leaf*, *house*, *hat*, *foot*. Have children circle each picture in the first box whose name begins with the /h/ sound. Then have children listen and point as you name the pictures in the second box: *kitten*, *king*, *key*, *turtle*, *flower*, *kite*. Have children circle each picture in the second box whose name begins with the /k/ sound.

Lesson 24

WORDS TO KNOW

he

no

1. Dan has no pet.

2. He has no dog.

3. Can he get a pet? Yes!

4. Will he get a dog?

Point to the words *he* and *no* and have children read them aloud. Do sentence 1 with children. Have them trace the word *no* and read the sentence aloud. Children complete 2, 3, and 4 on their own.

Comprehension

Draw Conclusions

Have children color the picture that shows Pumpkin. Then have children draw a picture that shows where Erin is.

Phonemic Awareness

Letters *Hh*, *Kk*

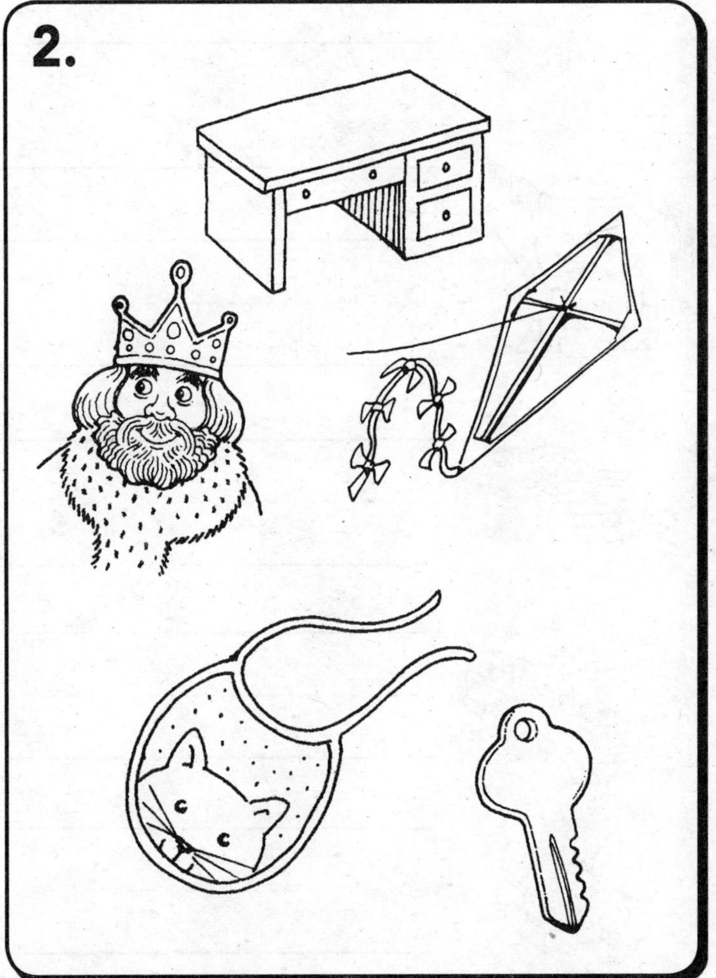

Name the pictures in the first box: *house*, *guitar*, *hat*, *logs*, *horse*. Have children color the pictures whose names begin with /h/. Name the pictures in the second box: *desk*, *king*, *kite*, *bib*, *key*. Have children color the pictures whose names begin with /k/.

Phonics

Letters *Hh*, *Kk*

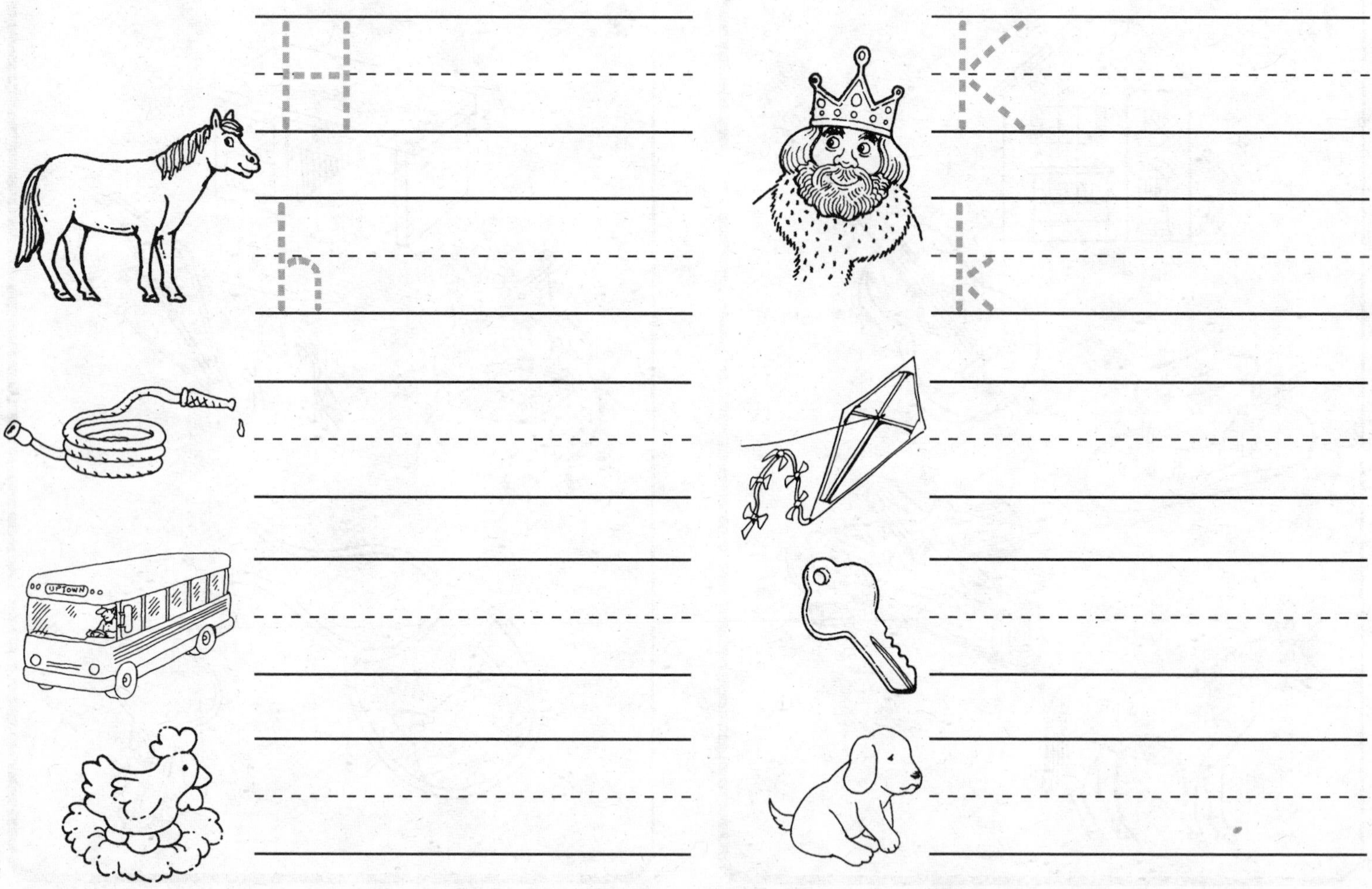

Point to and name each picture: *horse*, *hose*, *bus*, *hen*, *king*, *kite*, *key*, *puppy*. Have children practice writing capital *H* and small *h*. Then tell them to write *Hh* beside the pictures whose names begin with /h/. Have children practice writing capital *K* and small *k*. Tell them to write *Kk* beside the pictures whose names begin with /k/.

Blend Phonemes

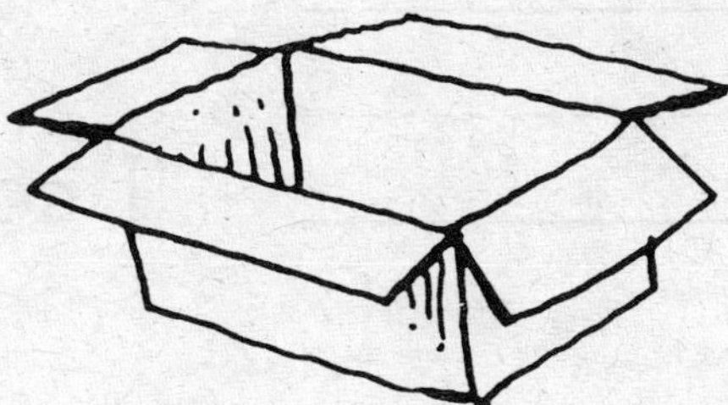

Tell children to listen as you say the sounds in one of the picture names: /b/ /ŏ/ /ks/. Have children blend the sounds, say the word, and color the box. Repeat for *pot*, *mop*, *top*, and *jam*. Have children use a different color for each object.

Lesson 25

WORDS TO KNOW

make
play
said
good
she
all
he
no

1. "I __________ the ," she said.

2. He is __________ on the .

3. She __________, "I can play the ."

4. I said, "We __________ play [ ]."

Have children read aloud the **Words to Know**. Read sentence 1 together. Have children choose the correct word, write it on the line, and then read the sentence aloud. Work with them to complete sentences 2–4. Have them draw a picture in the box that shows something they can all play.

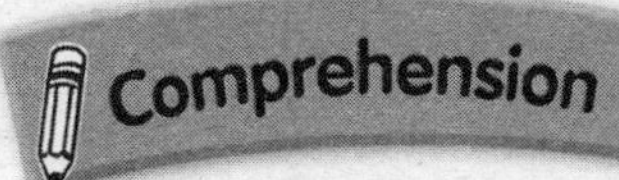

Text and Graphic Features

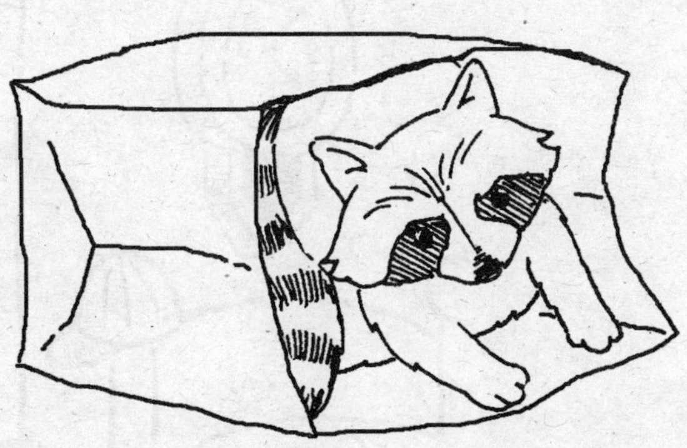

After listening to the story about the raccoon, have children circle the raccoon playing with a paper bag. Have them discuss and then color the pictures that tell more information about raccoons.

Phonemic Awareness

Blend Phonemes

Tell children you will say the sounds in the name of something they see in the picture: /r/ /ŭ/ /g/. Have children blend the sounds, say the word, and circle the object. Repeat with *dog*, *hat*, *ball*, *bed*, *bear*.

Blend Words

tip tan ten

net not nap

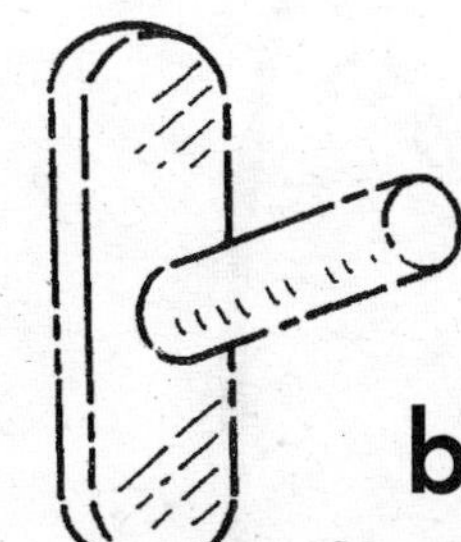

bag peg big

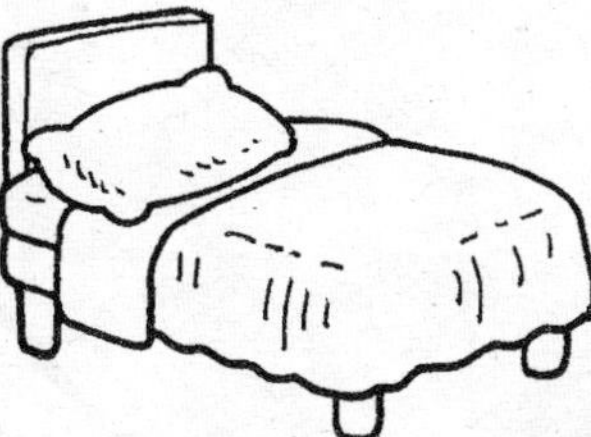

bad bed bid

Name the pictures: *ten*, *net*, *peg*, *bed*. Have children read the words beside each picture, circle the correct word, and write it on the line. Do the first one together.

Phonemic Awareness

Letter *Uu*

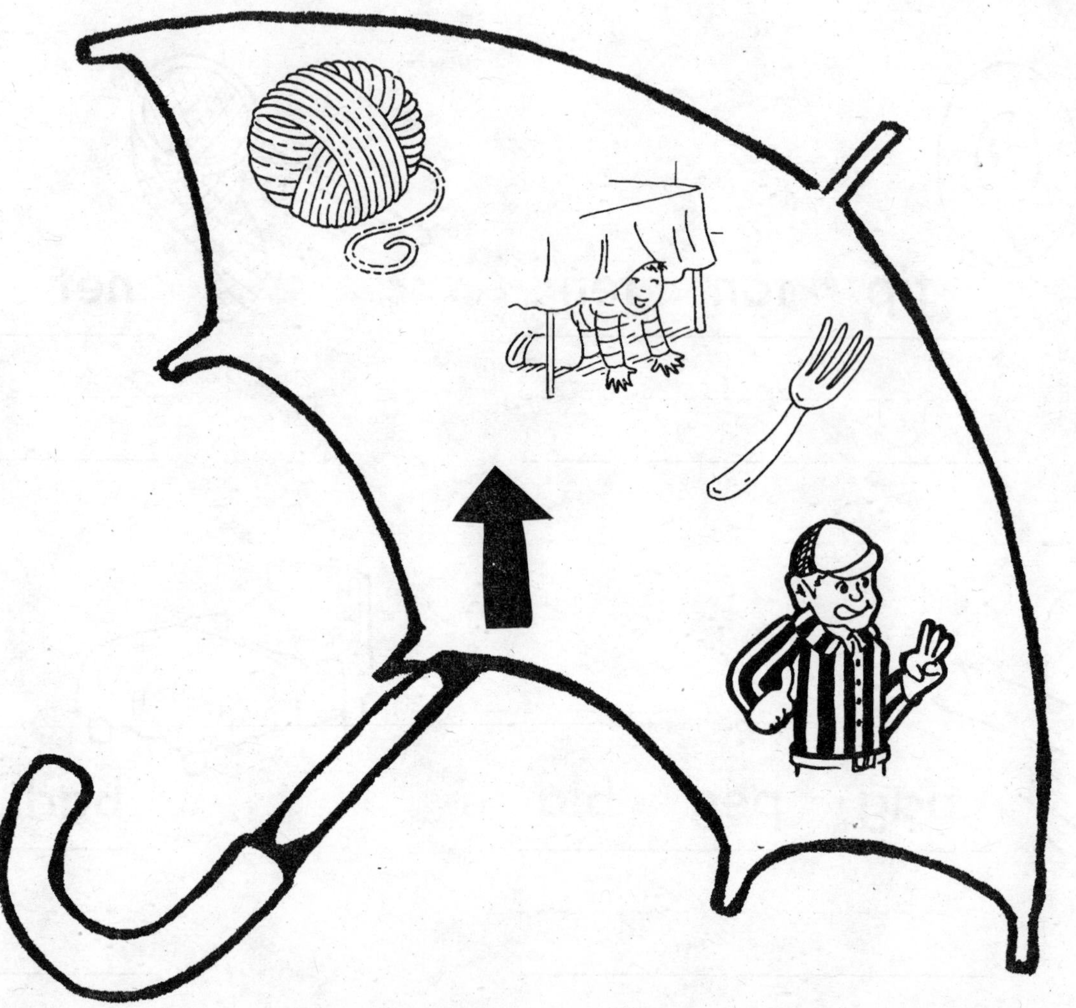

Have children point to the umbrella as you name it. Tell children to repeat the picture names after you: *umbrella*, *yarn*, *under*, *up*, *fork*, *umpire*. Have children color the pictures whose names begin with the same sound as *umbrella*.

Lesson 26

WORDS TO KNOW

do

down

1. What can she do ? She can 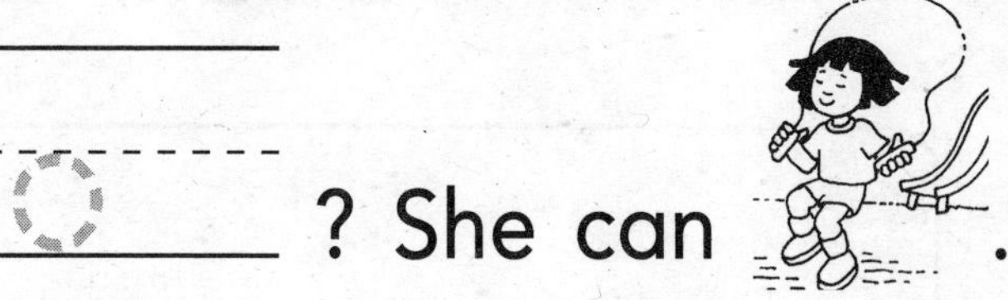 .

2. He can go down the .

3. What can he ______ ? He can 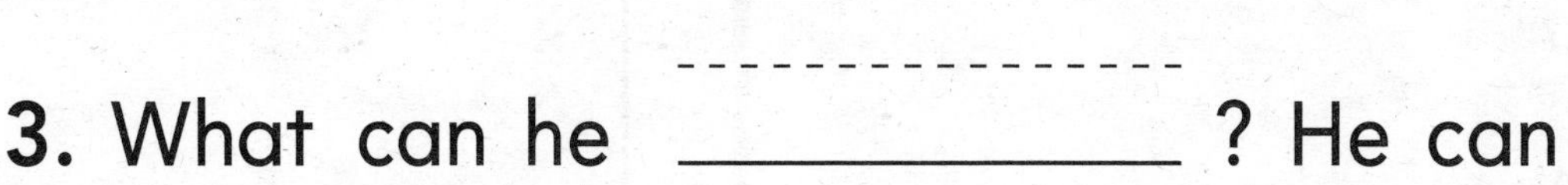 .

4. She will come ______ the 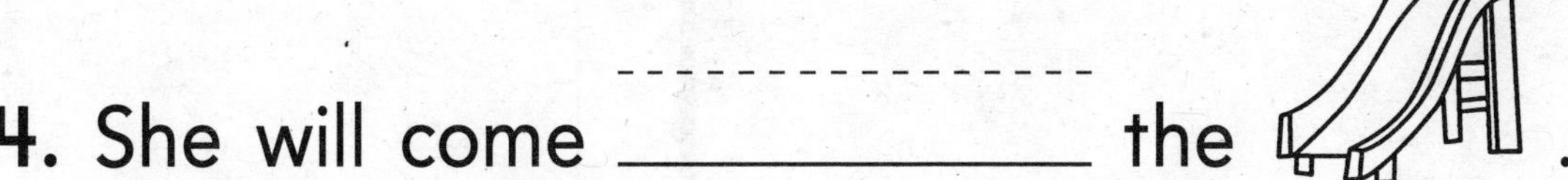 .

Have children read the words *do* and *down*. Complete sentences 1 and 2 with children. Have them trace the words *do* and *down* and read the sentences aloud. Children complete sentences 3 and 4 on their own.

Comprehension

Cause and Effect

Have children think about what happens in the story when Buddy smells the cat. In the left box, have them draw what the cat does in the story. In the right box, have them draw what causes the cat to do this.

Letter *Uu*

Have children point as you name the pictures: *bus*, *bun*, *tree*, *sun*, *fan*, *tub*. Have them say the word *bus* and listen for the middle sound /ŭ/. Have them color each picture whose name has the same /ŭ/ sound as *bus*.

Phonics

Letter *Uu*

Have children point to the rug as you name it. Have them say the middle sound /ŭ/ and practice writing capital *U* and small *u*. Then have children point to the other pictures as you name them: ***bus***, ***jug***, ***cat***, ***nut***. Have them write *Uu* next to pictures whose names contain the /ŭ/ sound.

Letters *Ll*, *Ww*

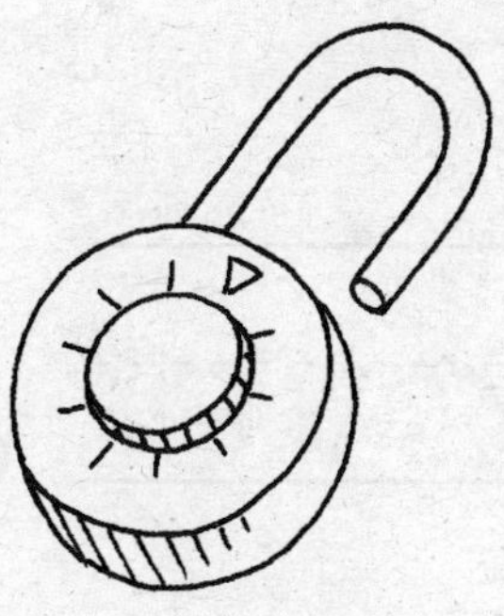

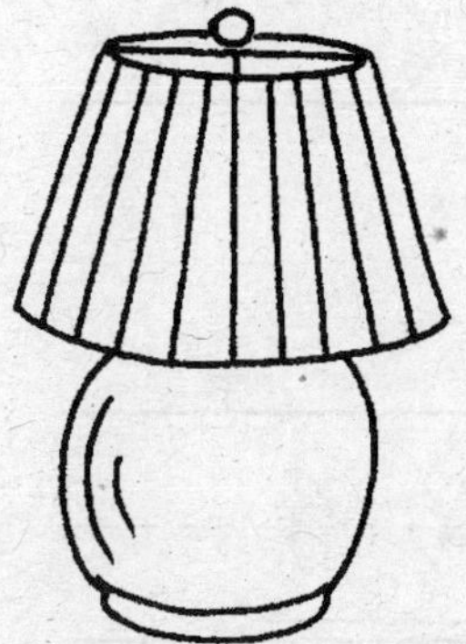

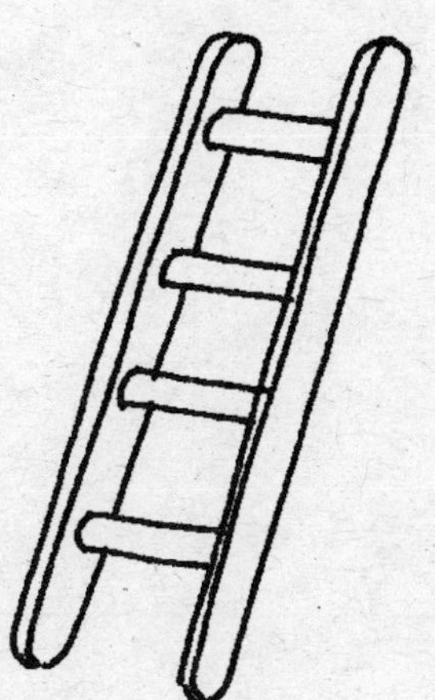

Have children point to the pictures as you name them: *web*, *lock*, *wig*, *wagon*, *lamp*, *ladder*. Have children point to the web and say the beginning sound /w/. Then have them color the pictures red whose names begin with /w/. Have children point to the lock and say the beginning sound /l/. Have them color the pictures blue whose names begin with /l/.

Lesson 27

WORDS TO KNOW

have

help

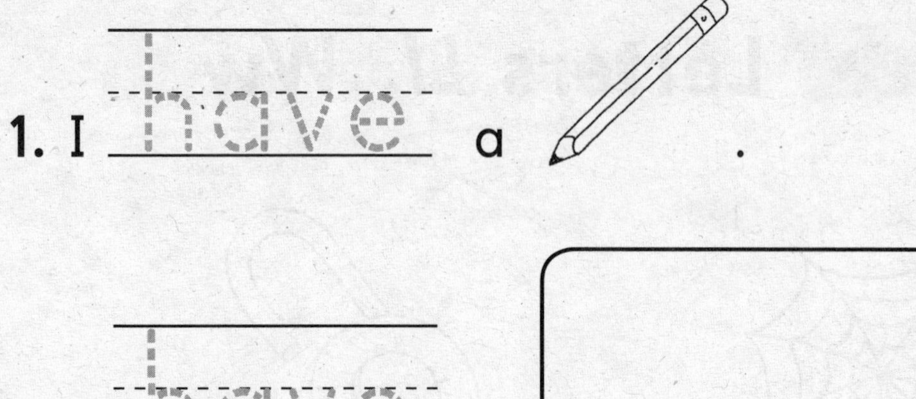

1. I have a .

2. I have a .

3. I help .

4. I help .

Have children read the words *have* and *help*. For sentences 1 and 3, have children trace the words and read each sentence aloud. For sentences 2 and 4, have children trace the words and draw a picture to complete each sentence. Then have them read their sentences aloud.

Comprehension

Compare and Contrast

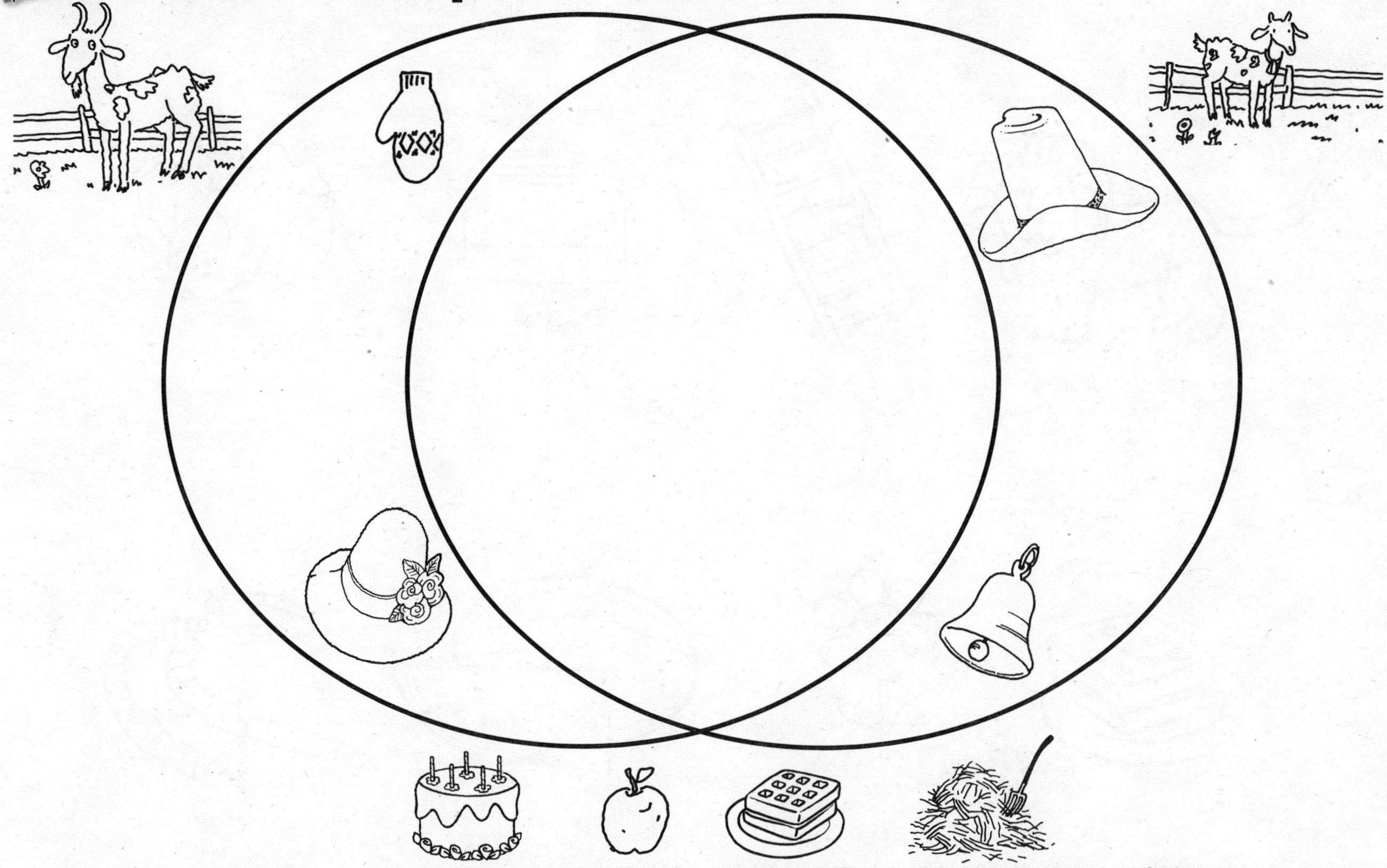

Explain that the Venn diagram shows how the goats in the story are the same and how they are different. The circle on the left contains things that describe Whippoorwill, and the circle on the right contains things that describe Choo-Choo. The middle is for things that describe both goats. Have children draw the items at the bottom of the page where they belong in the diagram.

Letters *Ll*, *Ww*

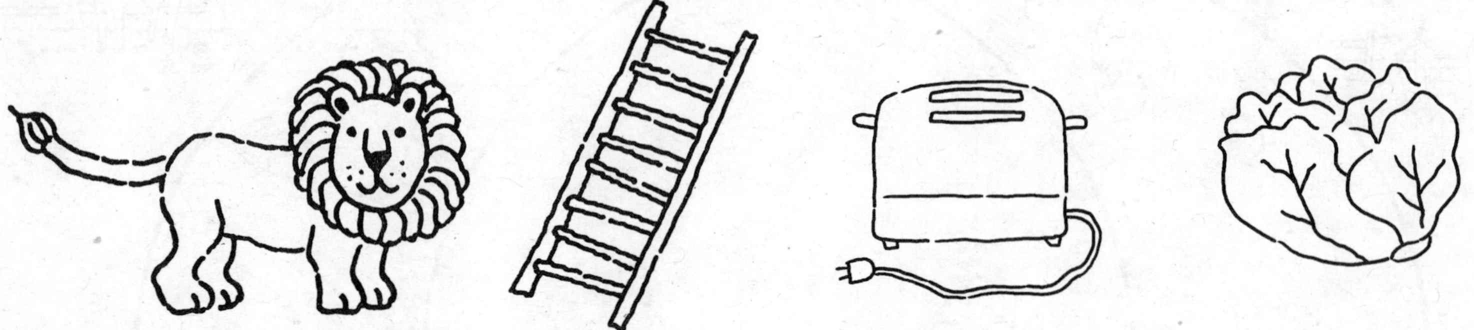

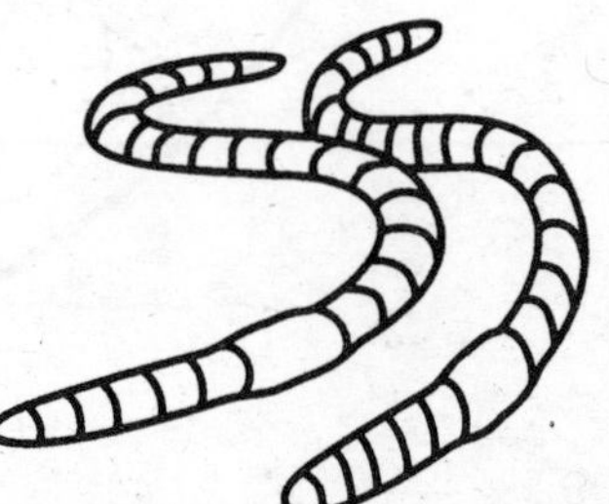

Have children point to the pictures in the first row as you name them: *lion*, *ladder*, *toaster*, *lettuce*. Then have them color the pictures whose names begin with /l/. Have children point to the pictures in the second row as you name them: *waffles*, *flower*, *watermelon*, *worms*. Then have them color the pictures whose names begin with /w/.

Phonics

Letters *Ll*, *Ww*

Have children point to each picture as you name it: *lemon*, *leaf*, *lizard*, *lips*, *waffles*, *watch*, *wagon*, *window*. Have children practice writing capital *L* and small *l*. Then have them write *Ll* beside the pictures whose names begin with /l/. Have children practice writing capital *W* and small *w*. Have them write *Ww* beside the pictures whose names begin with /w/.

Phonemic Awareness

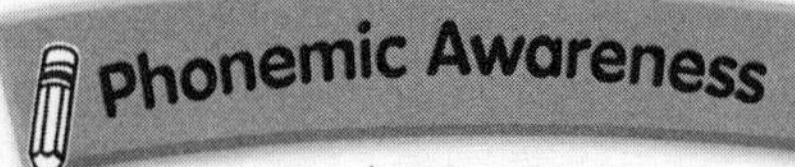

Letters *Vv*, *Zz*

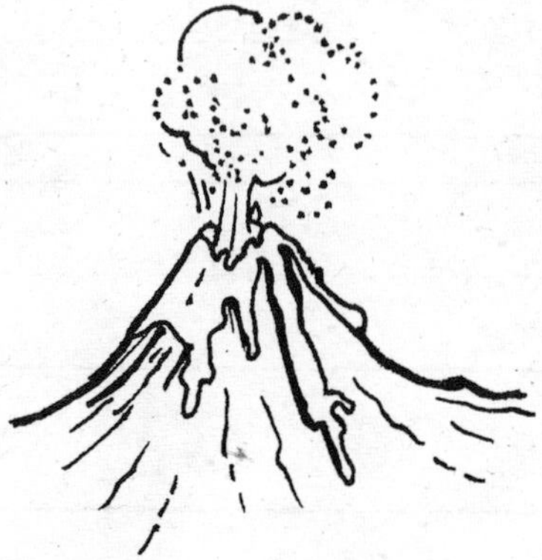
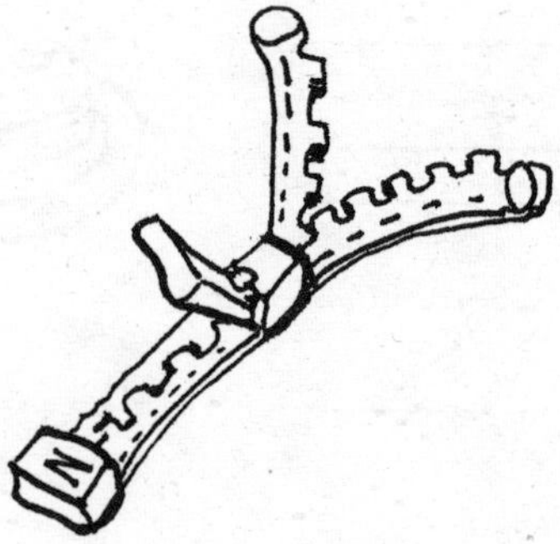
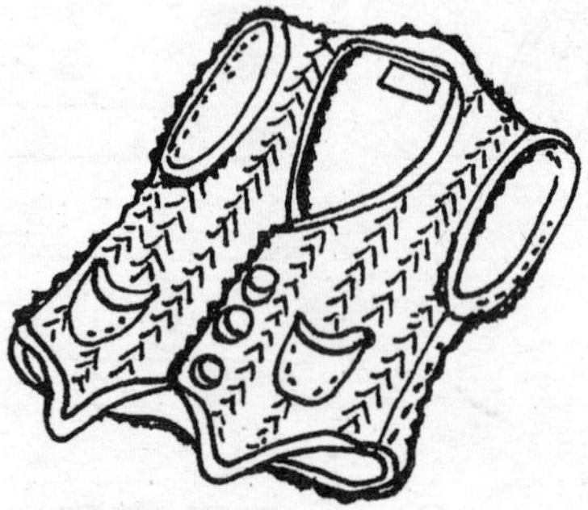
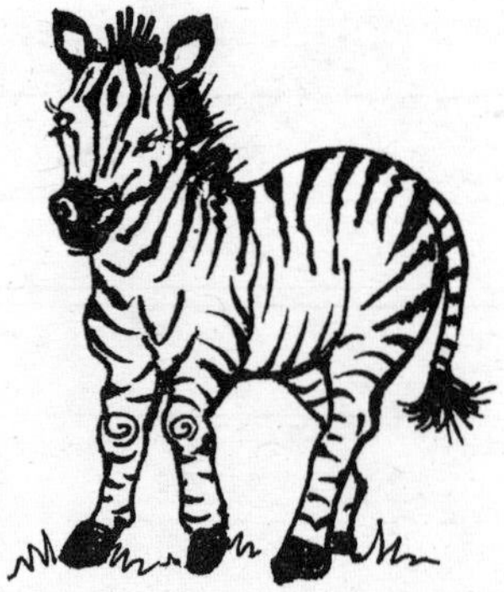
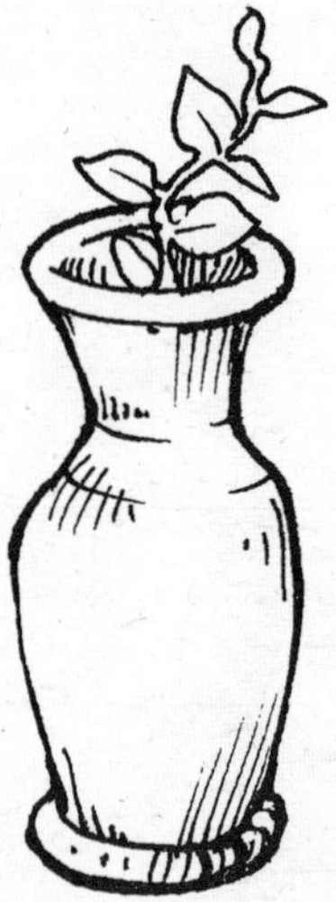
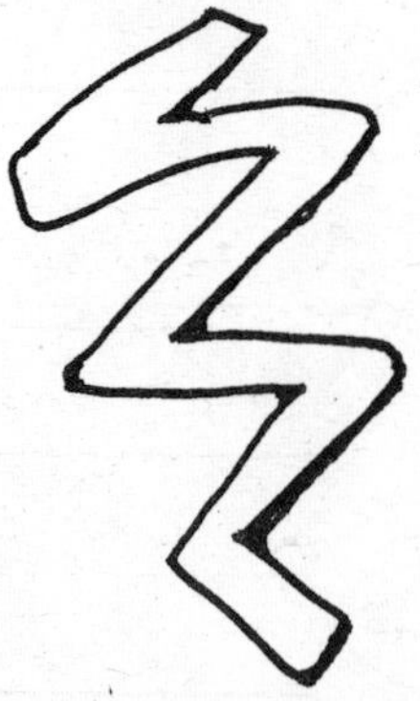

Have children point to the pictures as you name them: *volcano*, *zipper*, *vest*, *zebra*, *vase*, *zigzag*. Have children point to the volcano and say the beginning sound /v/. Then have them color the pictures yellow whose names begin with /v/. Have children point to the zipper and say the beginning sound /z/. Have them color the pictures green whose names begin with /z/.

Lesson 28

✓ WORDS TO KNOW

look

out

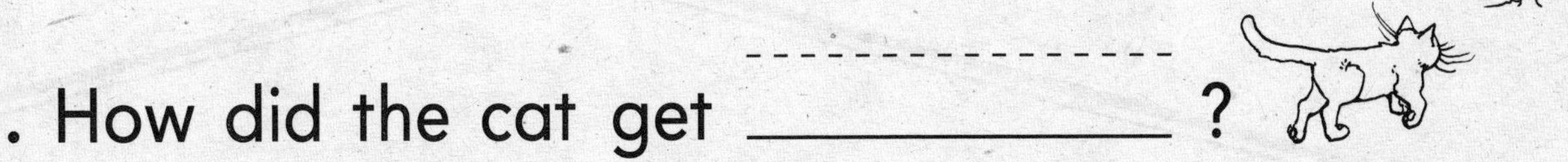

1. How did the cat get ________ ?

2. Help me ________ for my cat.

3. Set ________ a box for the cat.

4. Now ________ in the box.

Have children read the words *look* and *out*. Read sentence 1 with children. Have them write the correct word to complete the sentence. Then have children read the completed sentence aloud. Continue with sentences 2–4.

Comprehension

Story Structure

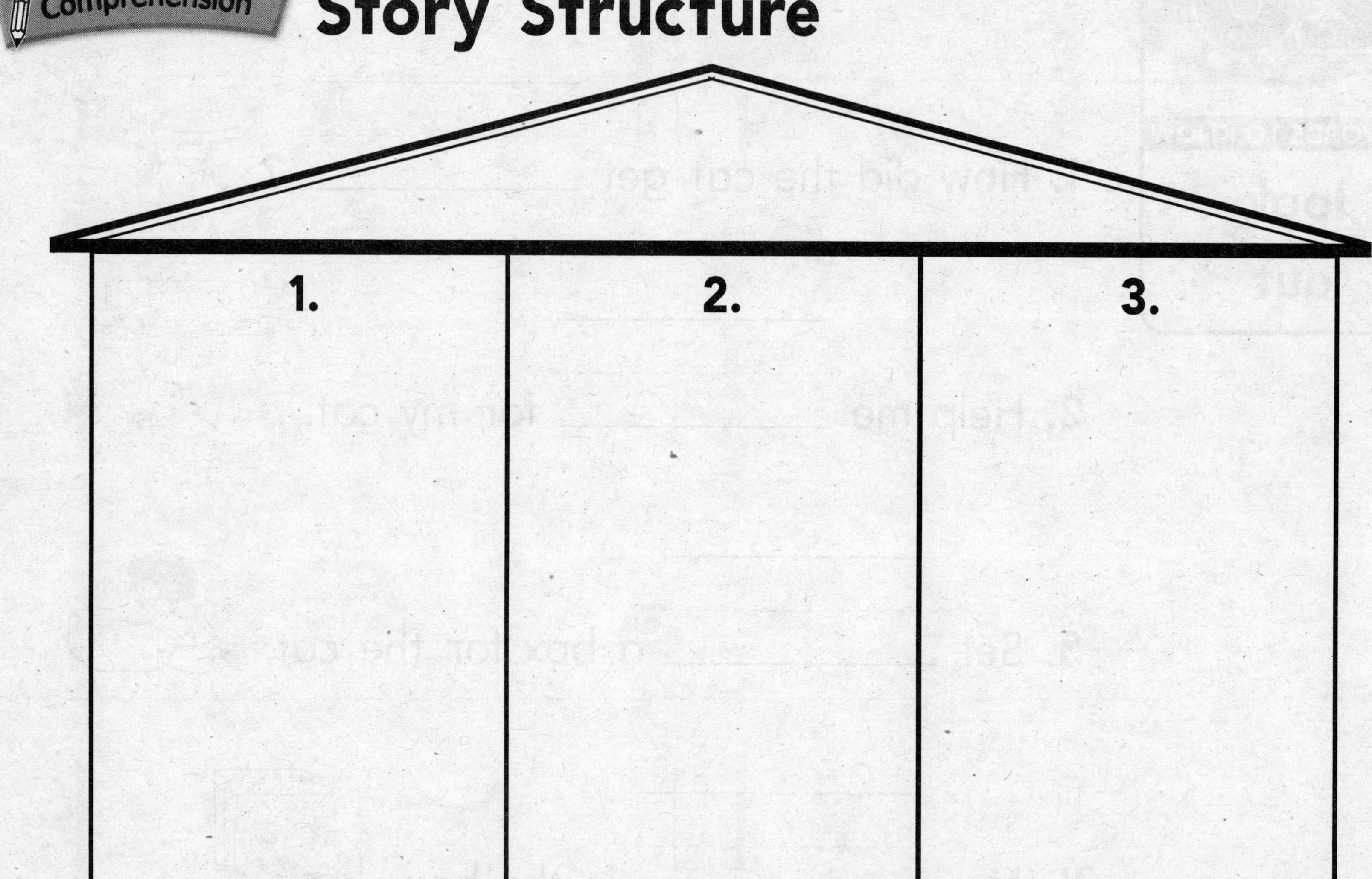

Have children use the first box to draw a picture of the characters in the story. Have them use the center box to draw where the story takes place and the third box to draw an important event from the story. Ask children to use their drawings to briefly retell the story.

Letters *Vv*, *Zz*

1.

2.

Have children listen and point to the pictures in the first box as you name each one: *van*, *volcano*, *vacuum*, *saw*, *cow*. Have children color each picture whose name begins with the /v/ sound. Then have children listen and point to the pictures in the second box as you name each one: *zebra*, *worm*, *zipper*, *zero*, *guitar*. Have children color each picture whose name begins with the /z/ sound.

Phonics

Letters *Vv*, *Zz*

Point to and name each picture: *violin*, *vest*, *vine*, *cake*, *zebra*, *zipper*, *zigzag*, *lion*. Have children practice writing capital *V* and small *v*. Then have them write *Vv* beside the pictures whose names begin with /v/. Have children practice writing capital *Z* and small *z*. Have them write *Zz* beside the pictures whose names begin with /z/.

Phonemic Awareness

Letters *Yy, Qq*

1.

2.

Have children listen and point to each picture in the first box as you name it: *yo-yo*, *yarn*, *yak*, *fish*, *lamp*. Have children color each picture in the first box whose name begins with the /y/ sound. Then have children listen and point to each picture in the second box as you name it: *quarter*, *bear*, *queen*, *question*, *quilt*. Have children color each picture in the second box whose name begins with the /kw/ sound.

Lesson 29

WORDS TO KNOW

off

take

1. We get off the bus.

2. We get off at the farm.

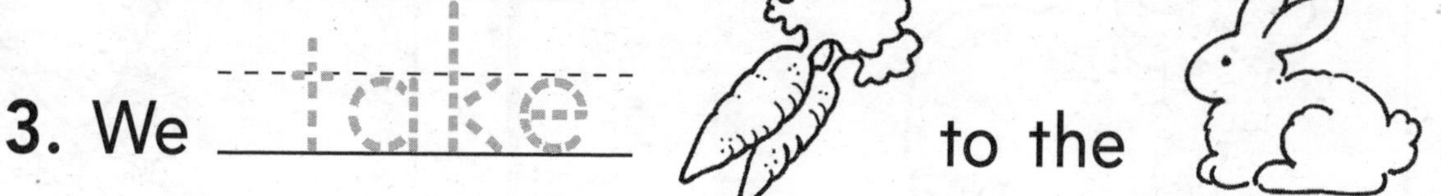

3. We take carrots to the rabbit.

4. We take apples to the horse.

Point to the words *off* and *take* and have children read them aloud. Complete sentence 1 with children. Have them trace the word *off* and read the sentence aloud. Name the picture in sentence 2: *farm*. Then have children trace the words in sentences 2–4 and read each completed sentence aloud.

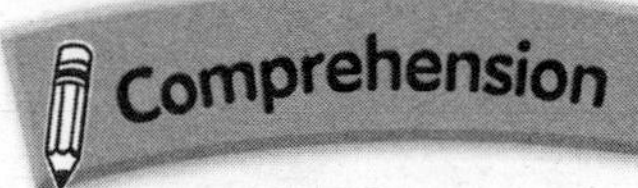

Main Idea and Details

1.

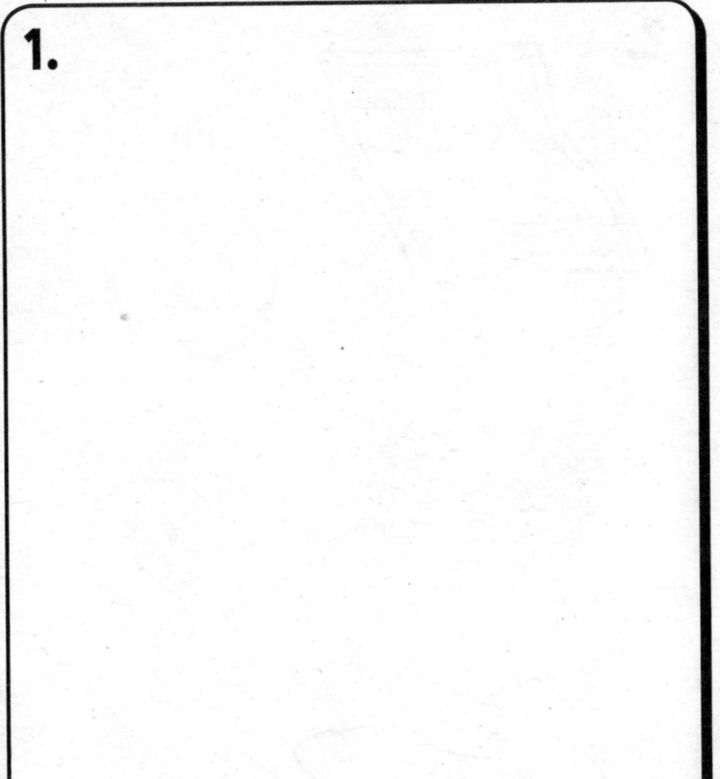

2.

Have children draw a picture for item 1 that shows the main idea in the story about Zachary's snowman. Then have children color the pictures in item 2 that tell more about the main idea.

Phonemic Awareness

Letters *Yy, Qq*

1.

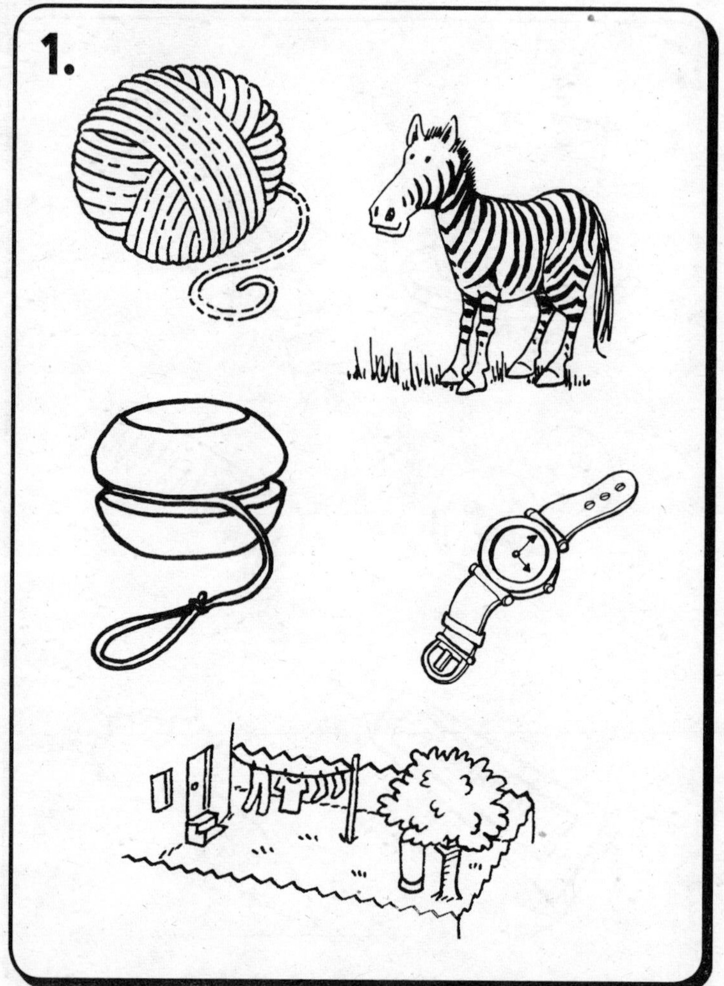

2.

Name the pictures in the first box: *yarn, zebra, yo-yo, watch, yard*. Have children color the pictures whose names begin with /y/. Name the pictures in the second box: *quilt, quarter, nest, question, hat*. Have children color the pictures whose names begin with /kw/.

Phonics

Letters *Yy, Qq*

Y

y

Q

q

Point to and name each picture: *yarn, yak, yawn, window, quilt, queen, turtle, quiet*. Have children practice writing capital *Y* and small *y*. Then have them write *Yy* beside the pictures whose names begin with /y/. Have children practice writing capital *Q* and small *q*. Have them write *Qq* beside the pictures whose names begin with /kw/.

Phonemic Awareness

Words with *a*, *e*, *i*, *o*, *u*

Name each picture: *bus*, *net*, *log*, *fan*, *wig*. Tell children to find the picture whose name has the /ă/ sound in the middle and color it green. Continue, having children identify the picture names with the sounds /ĕ/, /ĭ/, /ŏ/, and /ŭ/. Have children use a different color for each sound.

Lesson 30

✓ WORDS TO KNOW

do
down
have
help
look
out
off
take

1. Help me ____________ for Dan.

look take

2. Is Dan ____________ here?

do down

3. Dan got ____________ the bus.

help off

4. We can ____________ fun.

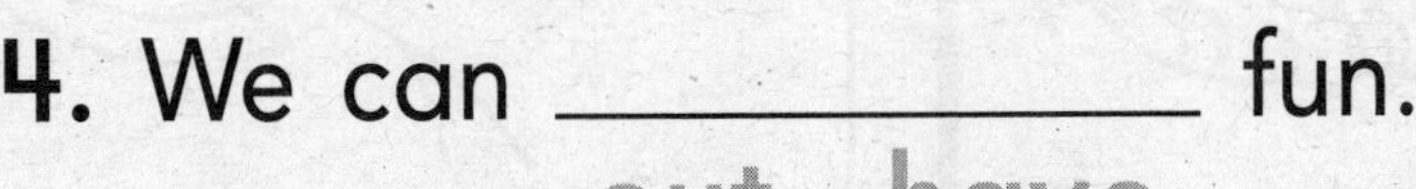

out have

Have children write the correct word to complete each sentence. For sentence 4, have children draw a picture to show something they can do to have fun.

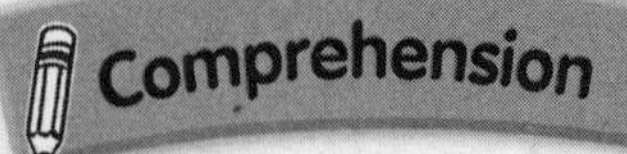

Understand Characters

Name the characters: *Miss Muffet*, *Dog*, *Kittens*, and *Jack*. Have children listen to nursery rhymes about the characters and then draw a face to show how each character feels.

Phonemic Awareness

Words with *a, e, i, o, u*

Say the names of the first pair of pictures: *jam/can*. Have children color the pictures if the names have the same middle sound. Repeat for the remaining picture pairs: *net/bed*, *fish/dog*, *box/doll*, *nut/mug*, *six/pig*.

Phonics

Blend Words

Name the pictures: *bus, sun, bat, mop, dig, leg.* Have children blend and read the words beside each picture, circle the word that matches the picture, and write it on the line. Do the first one together.

Phonemic Awareness

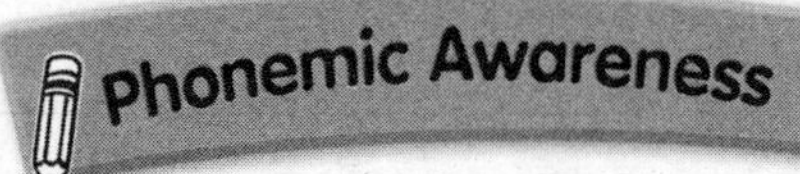

Track Syllables

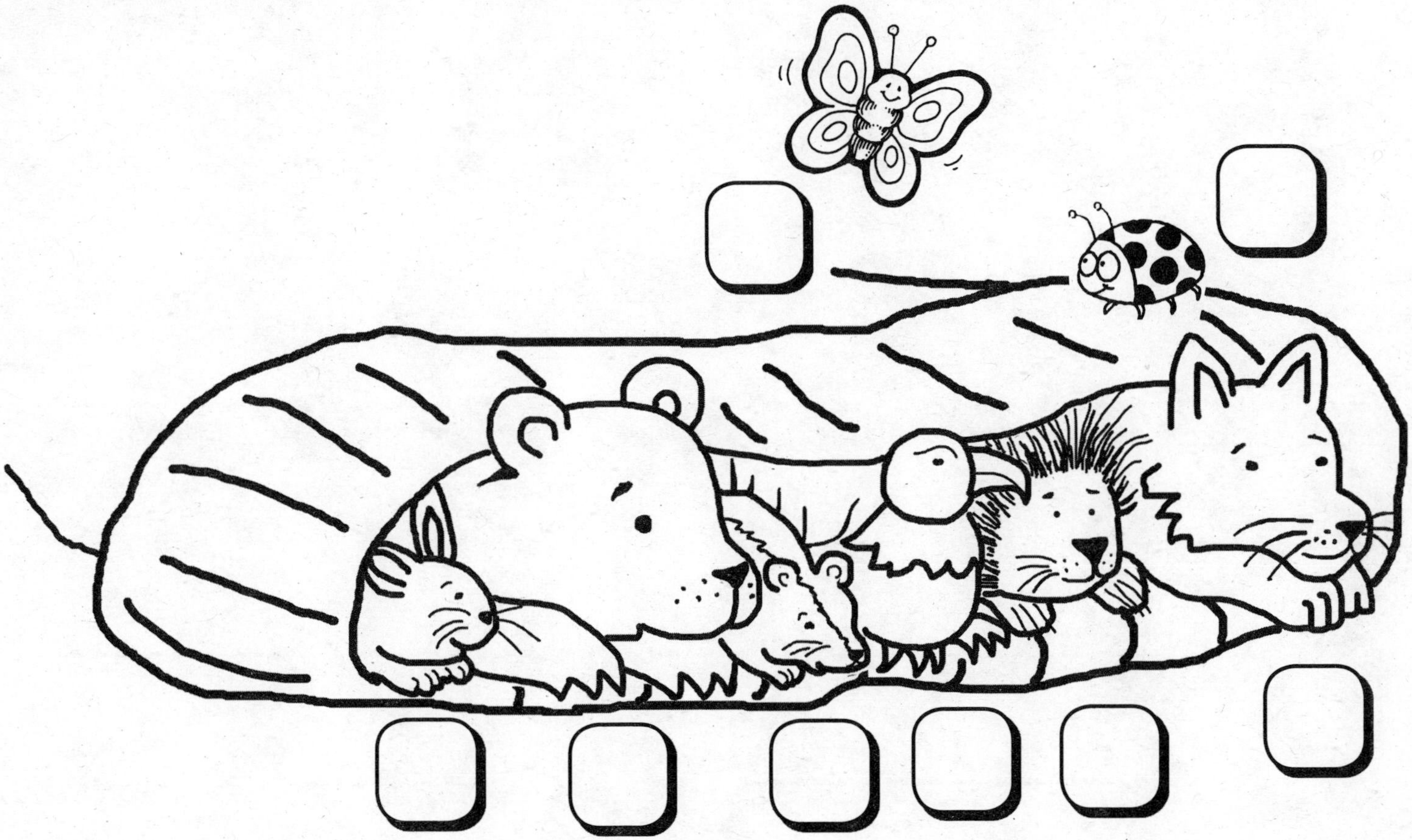

Have children point to the rabbit. Have them say *rabbit*, clap the syllables, and then write a 2 by the rabbit to show that the word has two syllables. Name the other animals: *bear*, *skunk*, *eagle*, *porcupine*, *wolf*, *butterfly*, and *ladybug*. Have children complete the page on their own.